It's roughly 100 miles from Monterey to Hearst Castle along Highway 1 in California, but what a drive. Winding roads and thousand foot cliffs accompany one throughout the trip and the extraordinary views make up for the length of the journey. During the last century and much so far of this one, artists and writers spent their time painting, sculpting, and writing of the extraordinary views of the sea, the waterfalls, the forests, and the history of the places there. Even now in winter, painters and authors far outnumber visitors who come to see the country that Henry Miller made famous along with Kim Novak, Elizabeth Taylor, Chevy Chase, Orson Welles, Richard Burton, and Rita Hayworth. In this collection of photographs of paintings of photographs mimicking styles of those that mimicked styles of those times, I have purposely kept the rendering low-resolution to help capture the essence of the period. None of the paintings herein are signed because they represent both various online and personal style algorithms rather than red-blooded crimes by the artists of the times.

The Artists
Of
Big Sur

Photographs
By
David Cope

The Artists of Big Sur
Photographs by David Cope

Epoc Books
Printed in the United States of America
© David Cope 2016
All Rights Reserved.
Published 2016.

This book is dedicated to my wife, sons, and grandchildren, Zoe, Tess, Gavin, and Ethan whose excitement for everyday things never ceases to amaze me. And to those older kids like me who believe in those children.

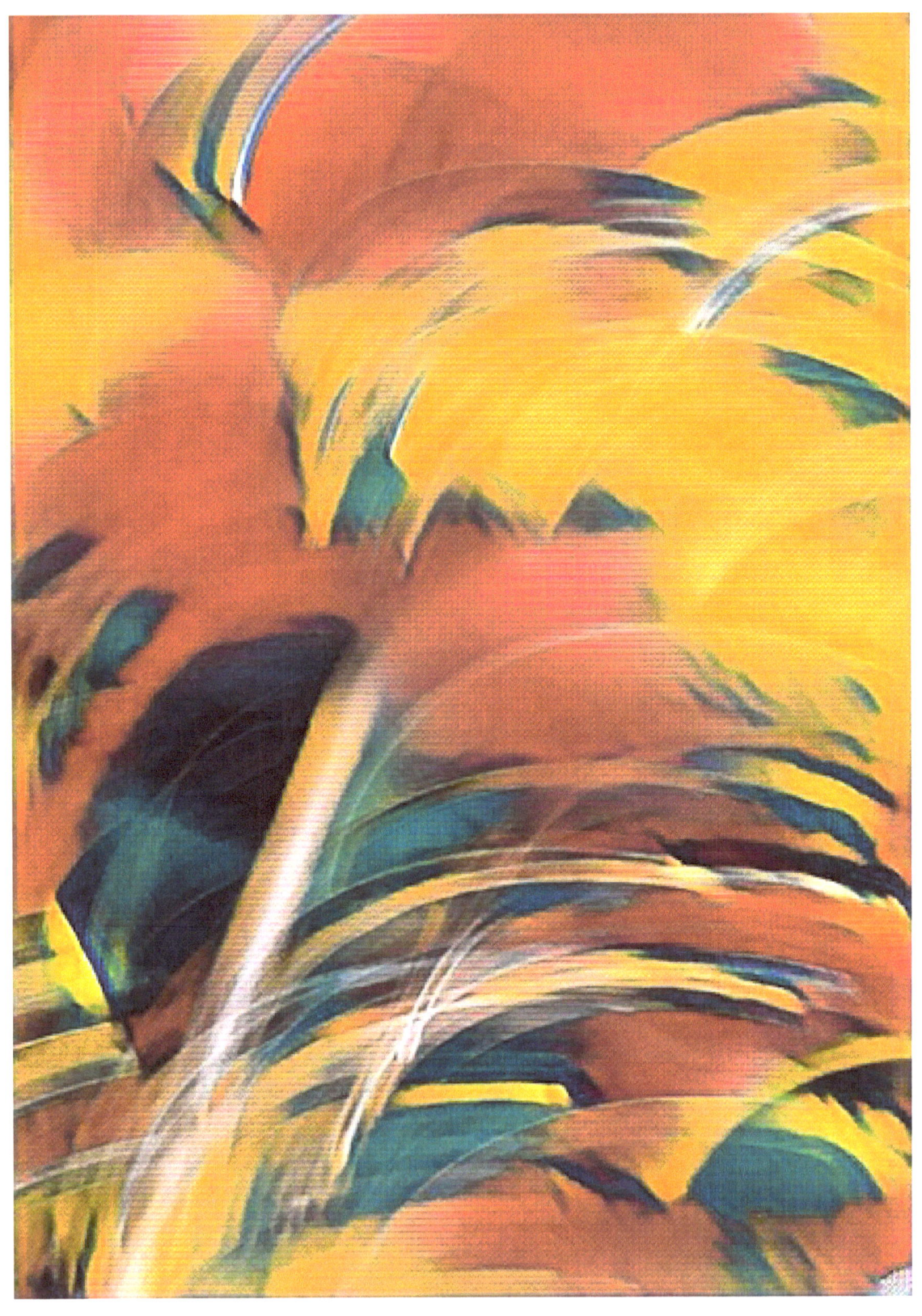

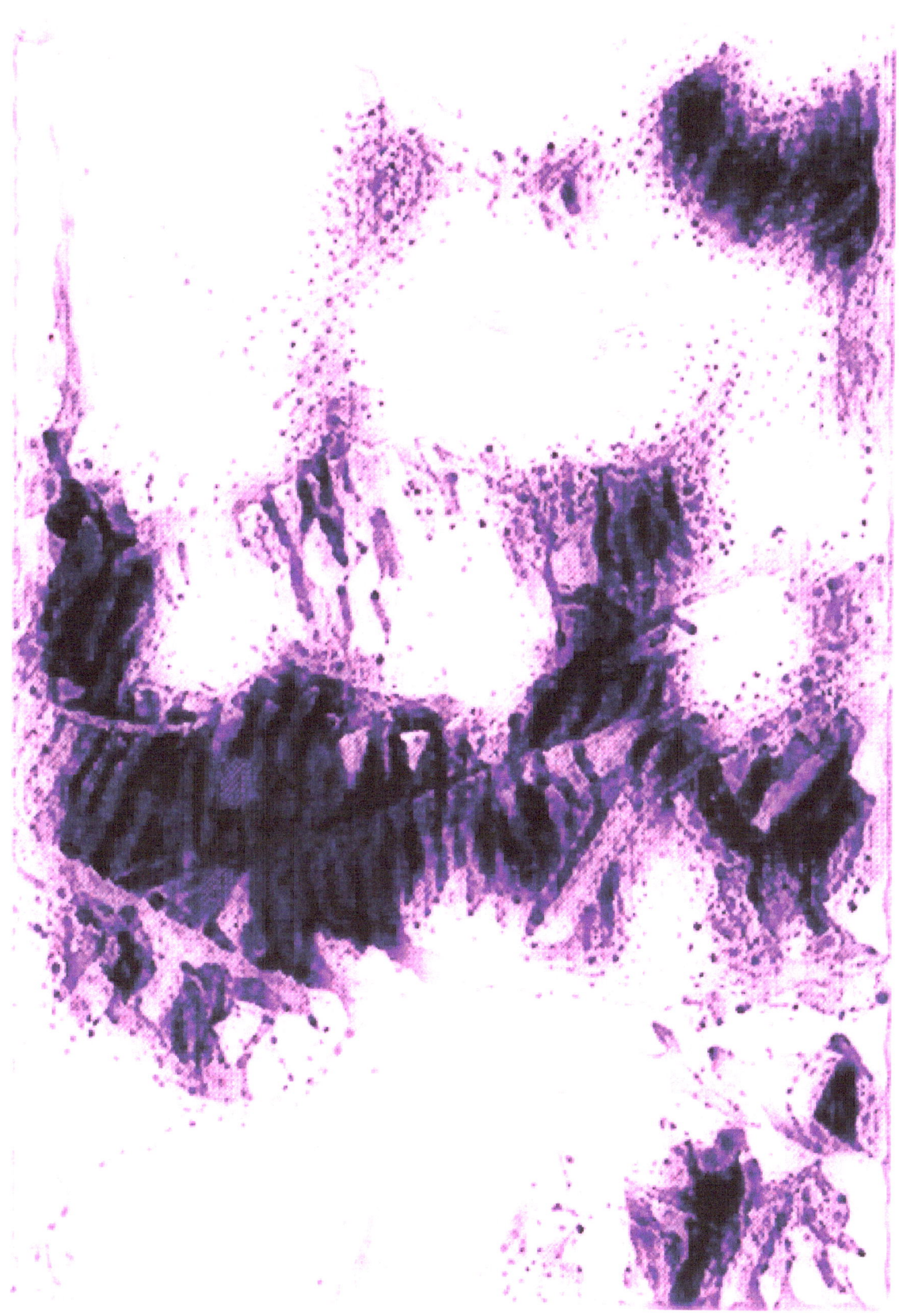

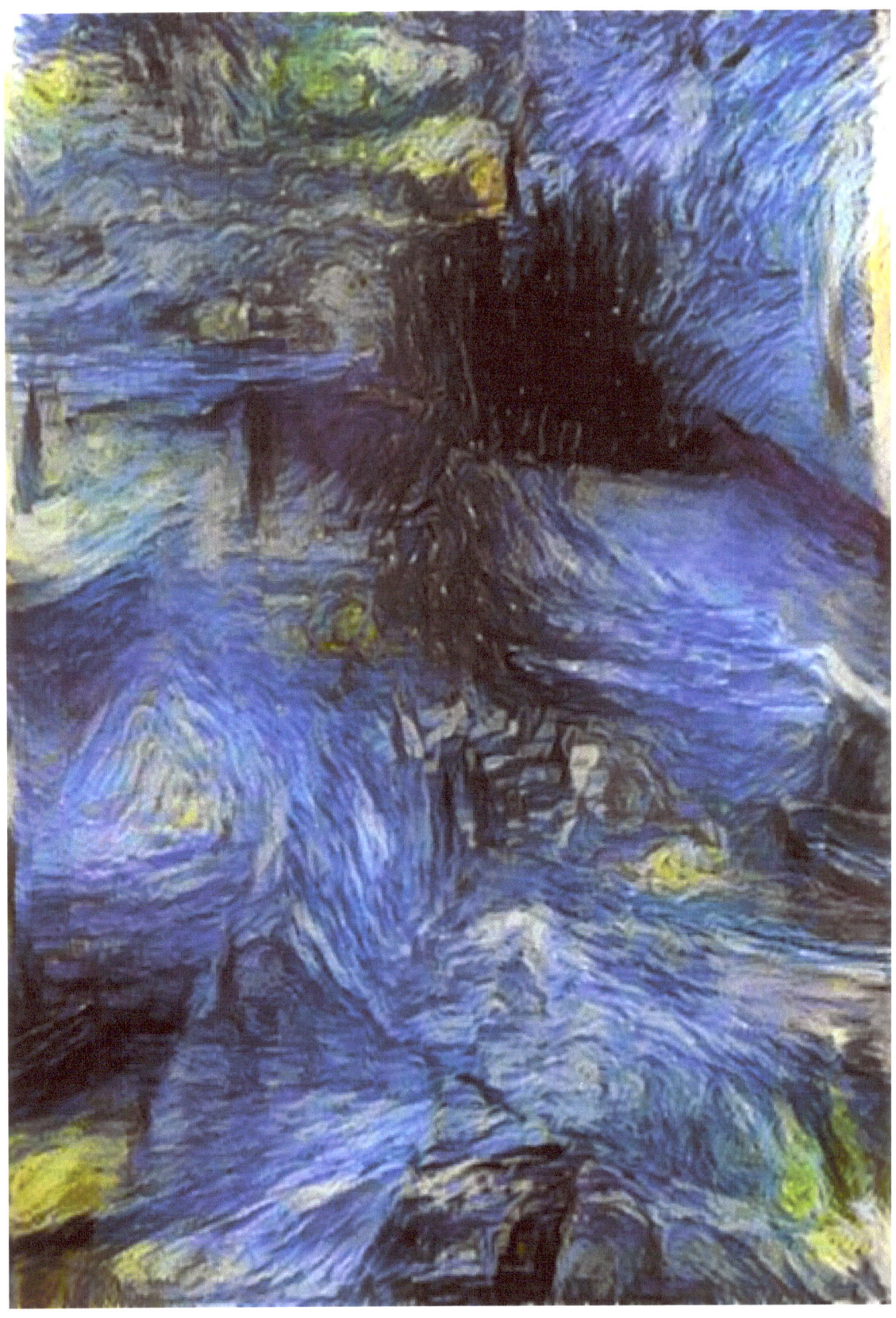

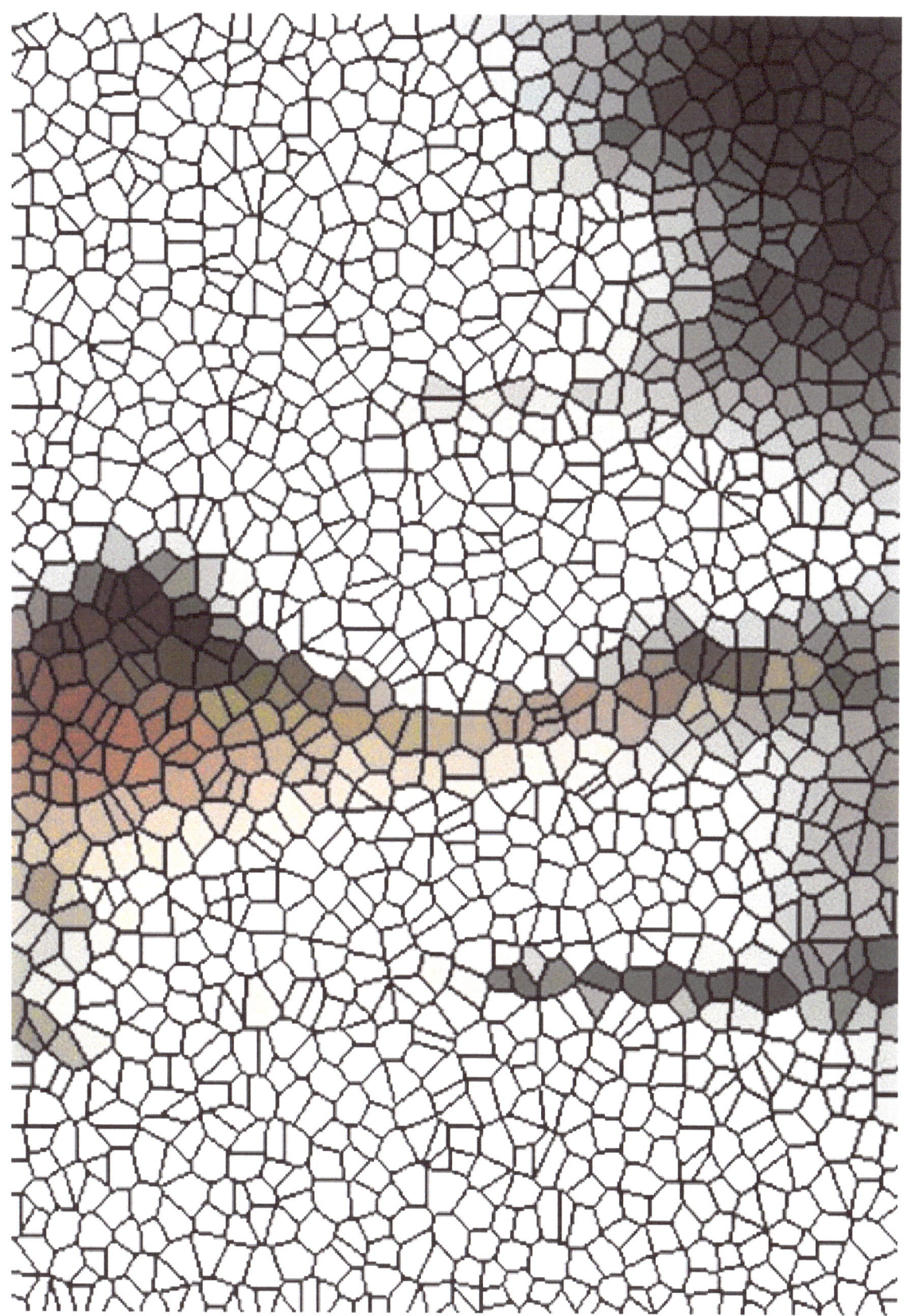

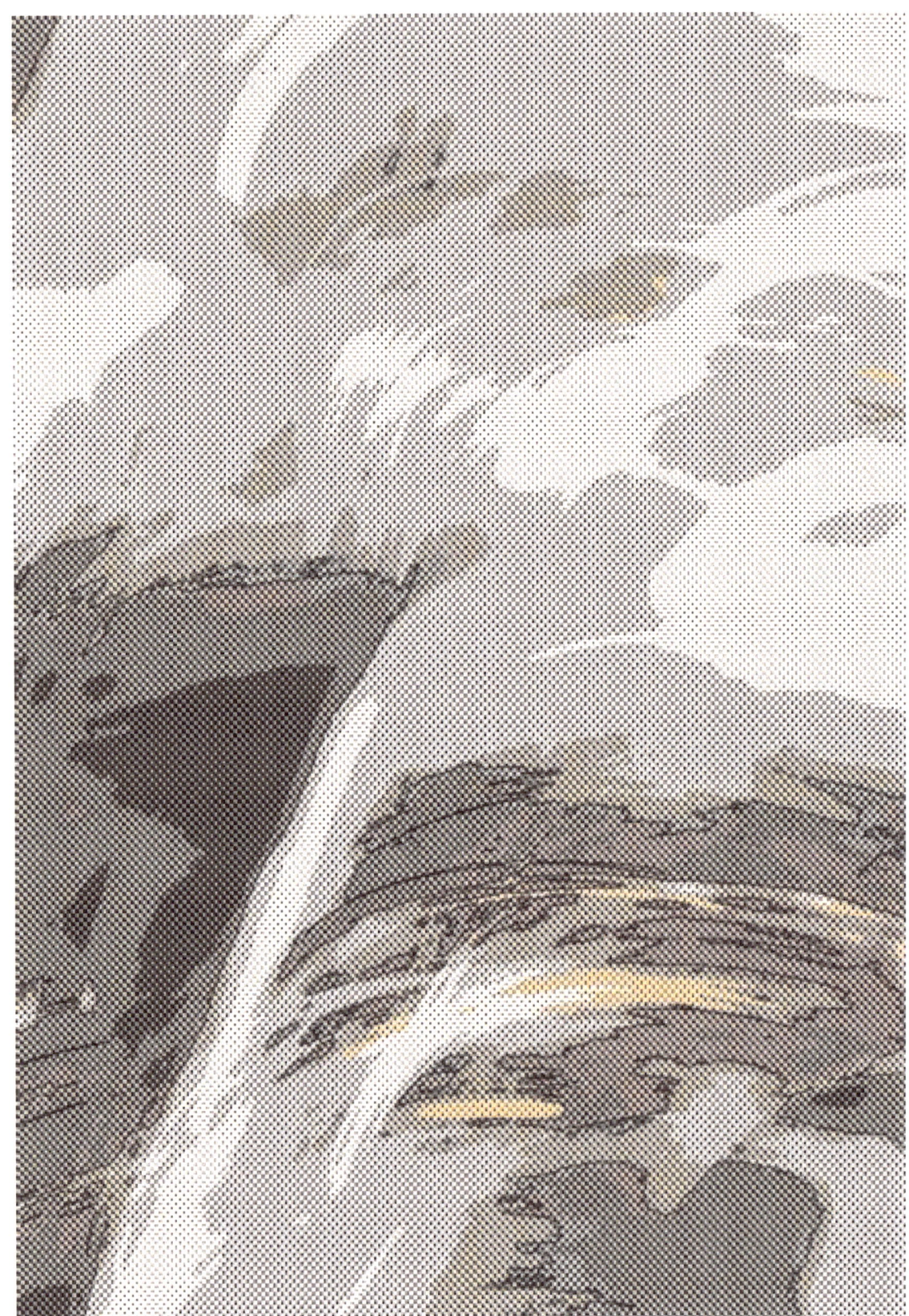

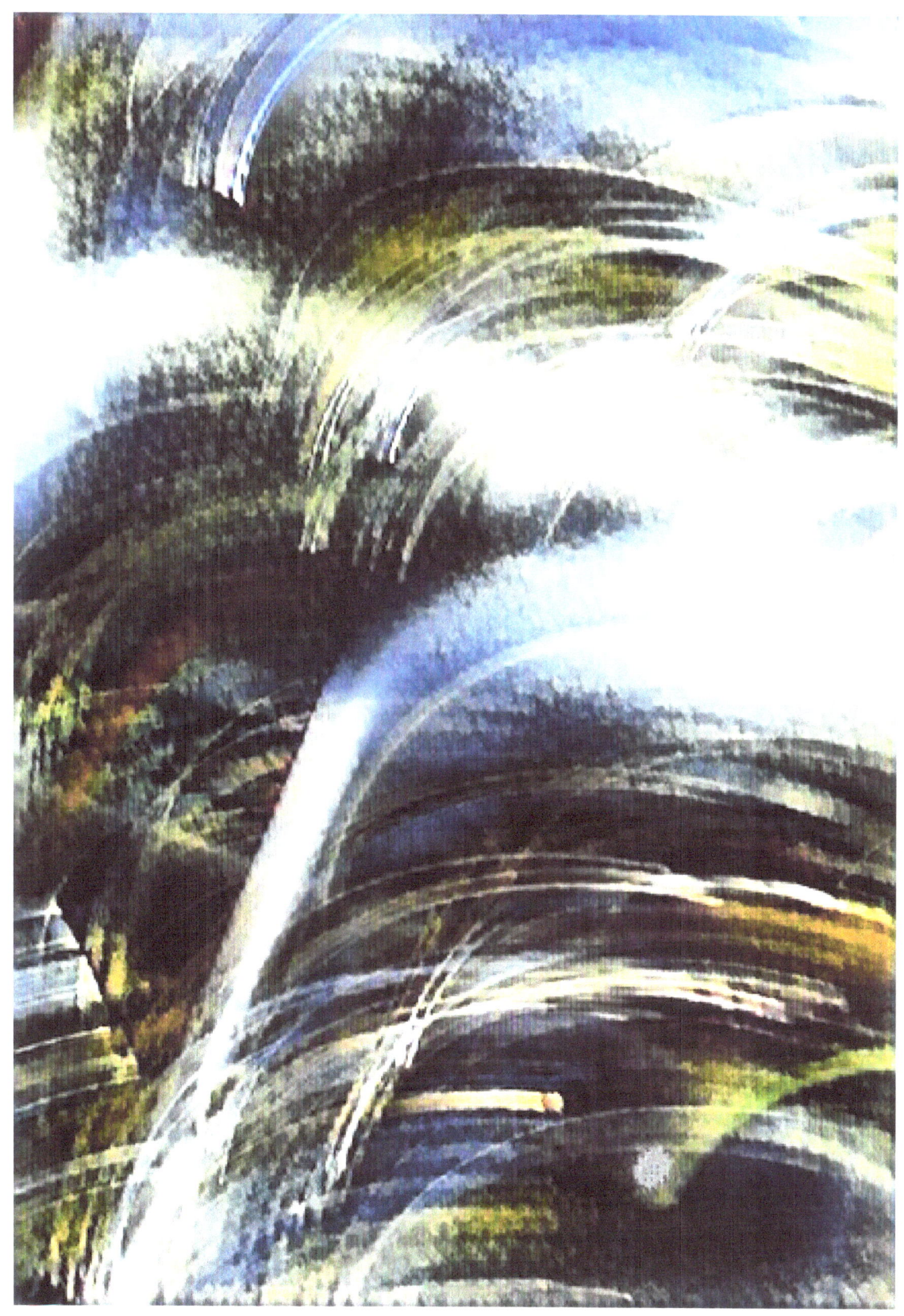

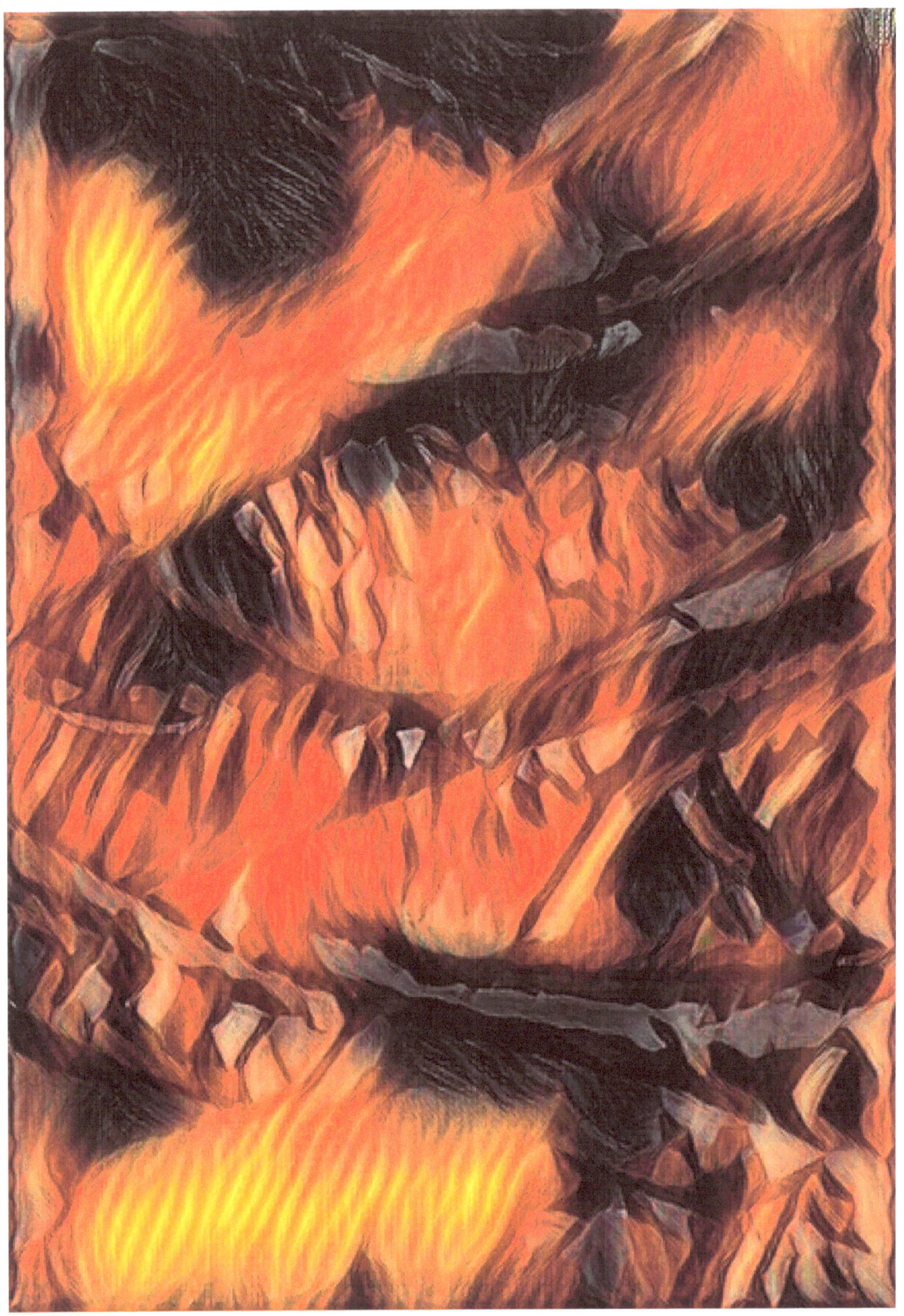

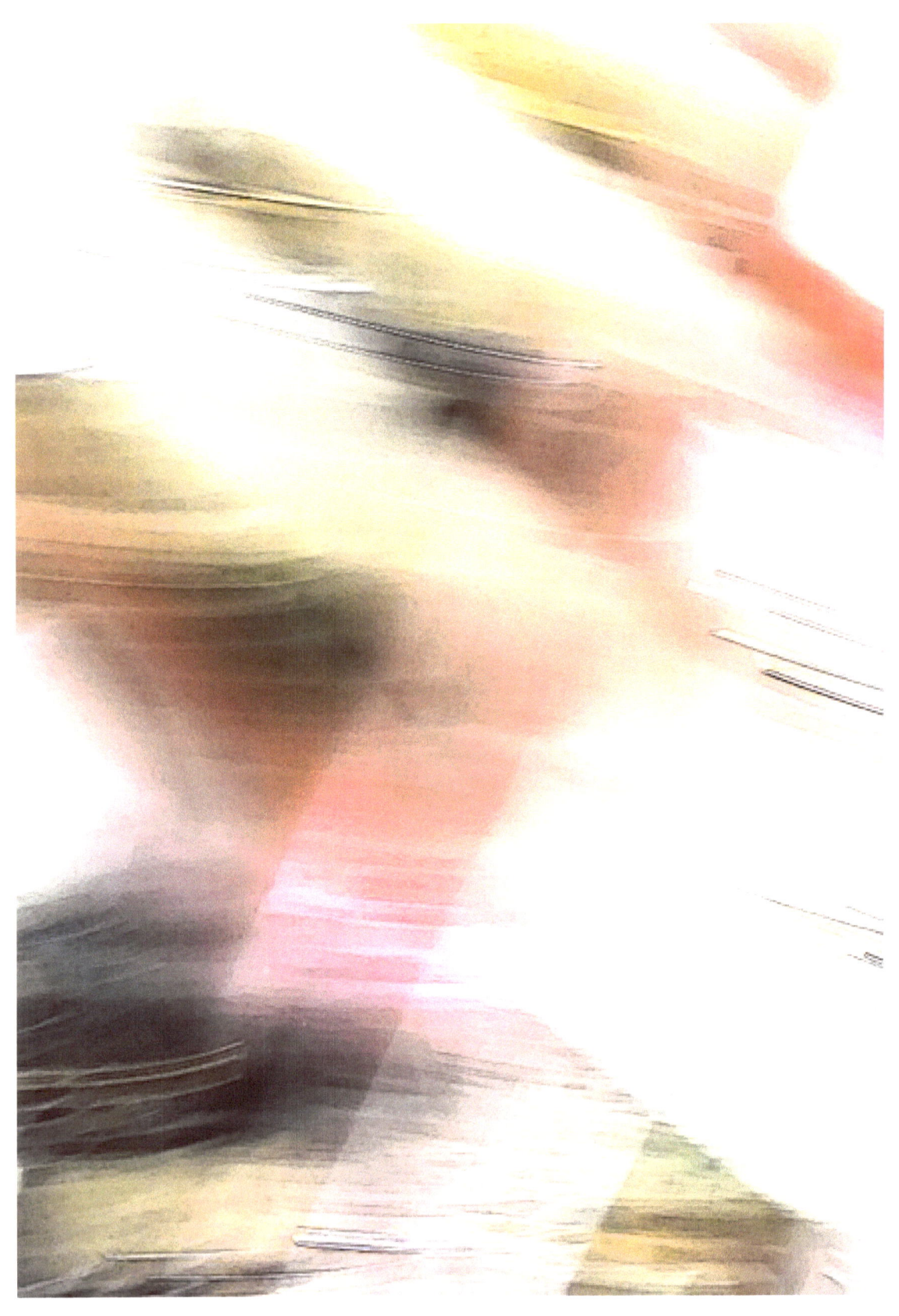

14

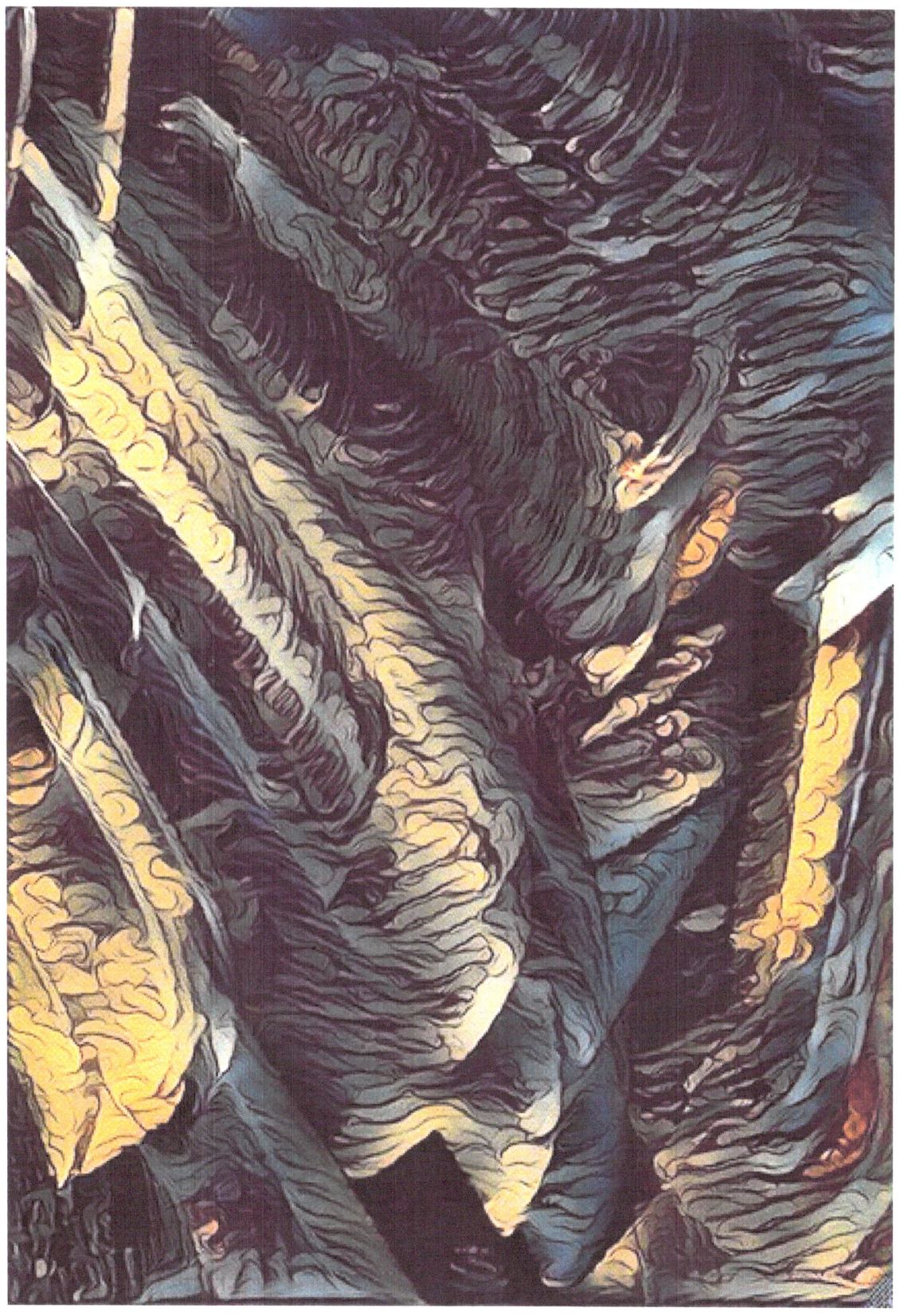

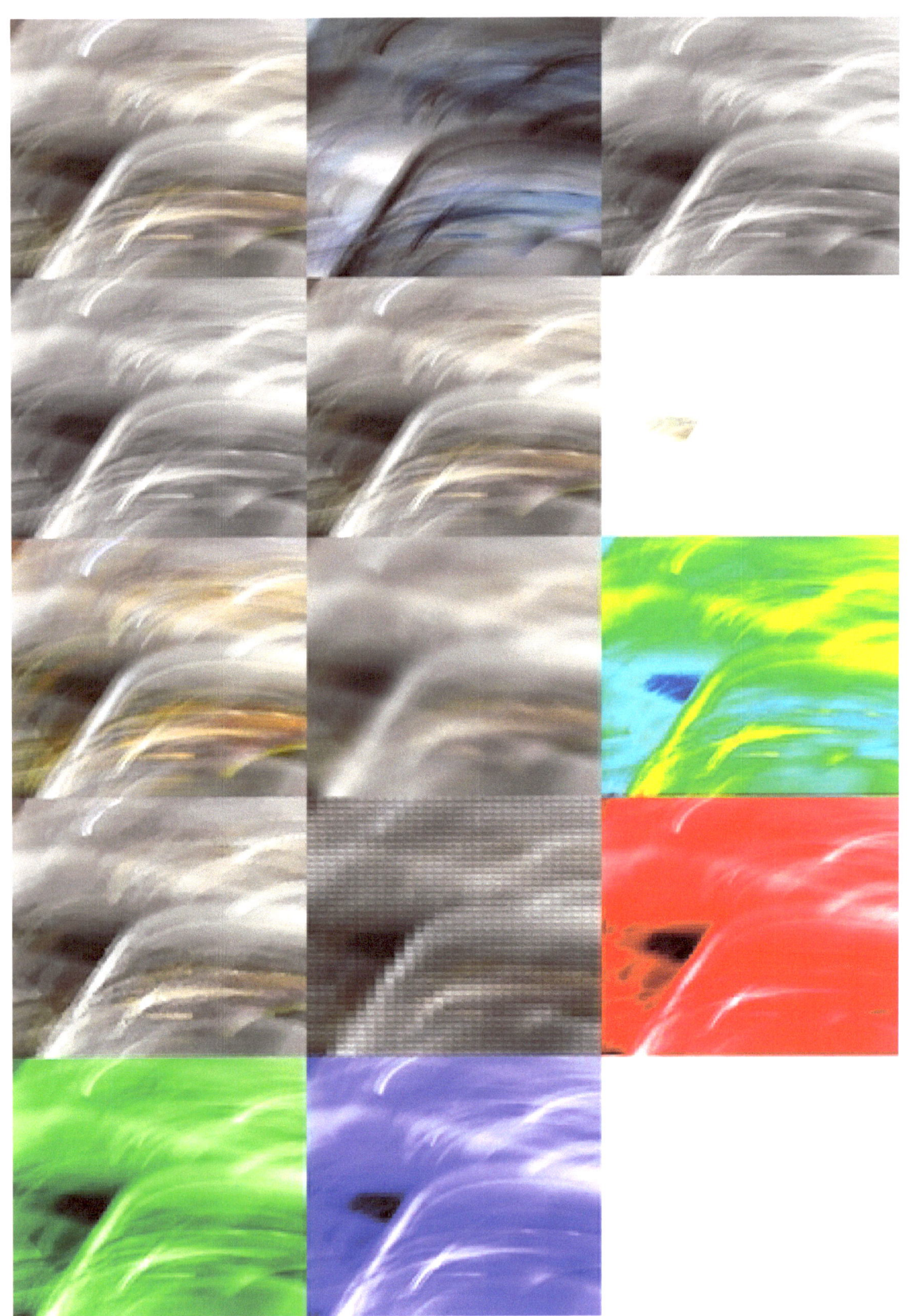

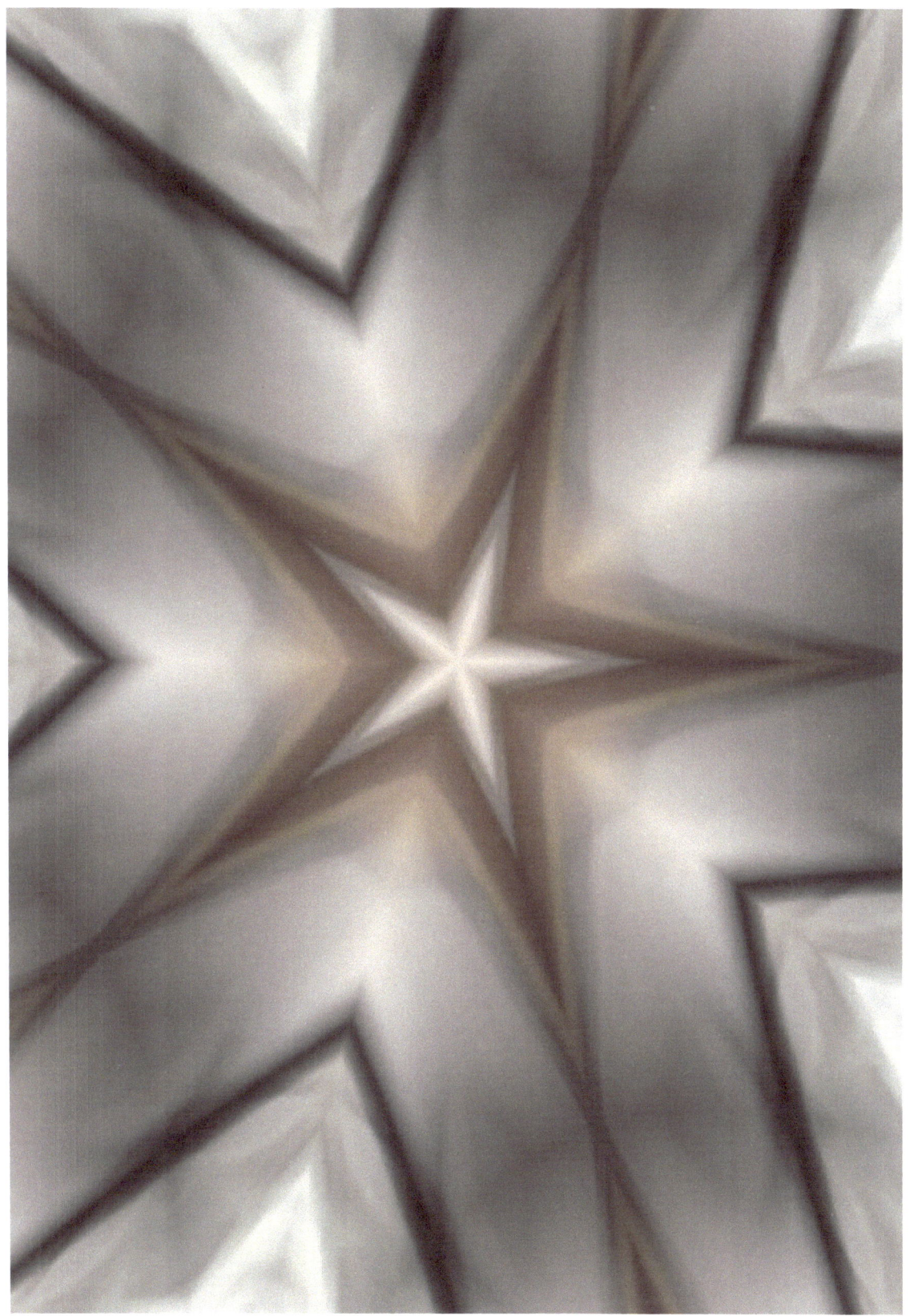

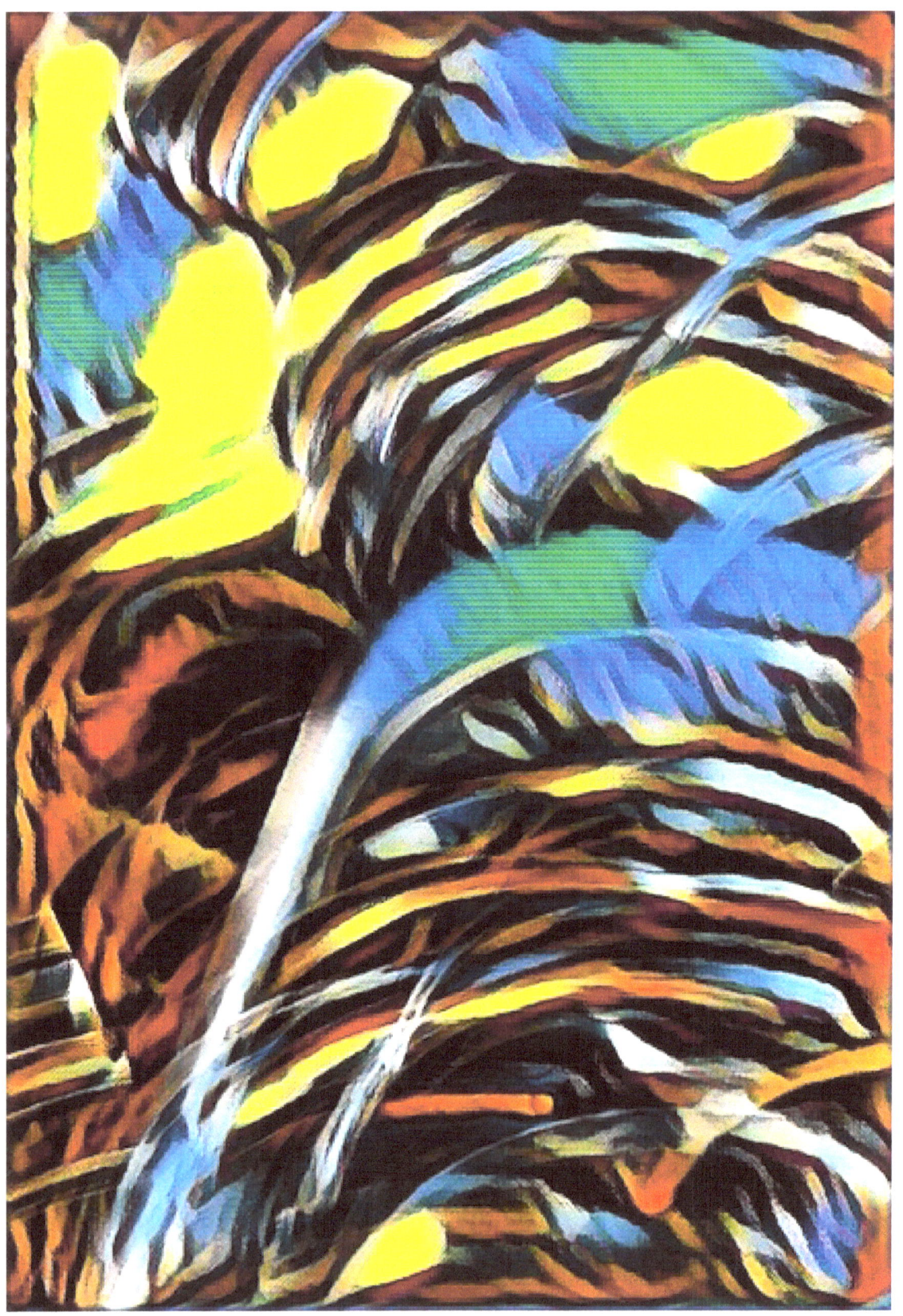

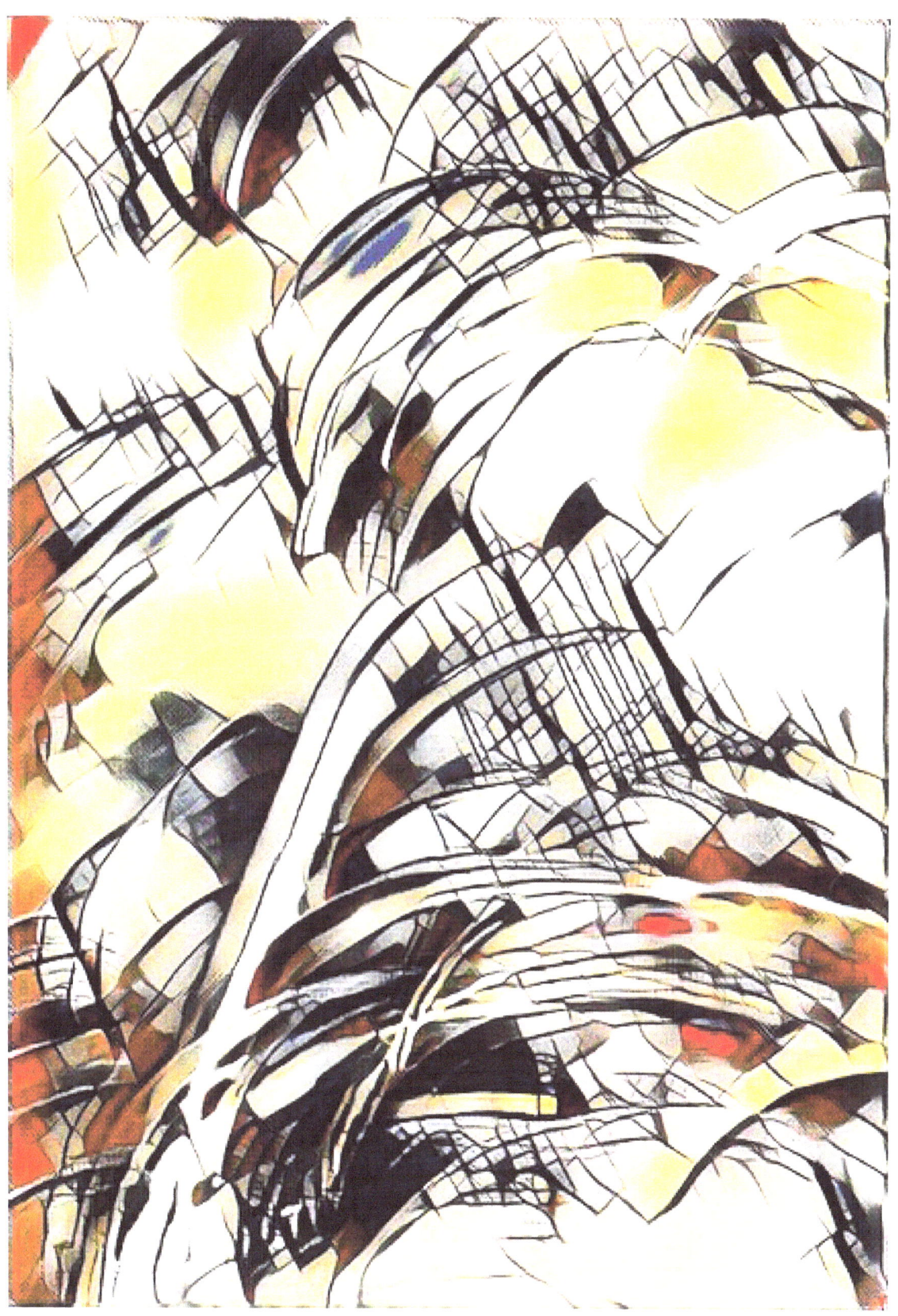

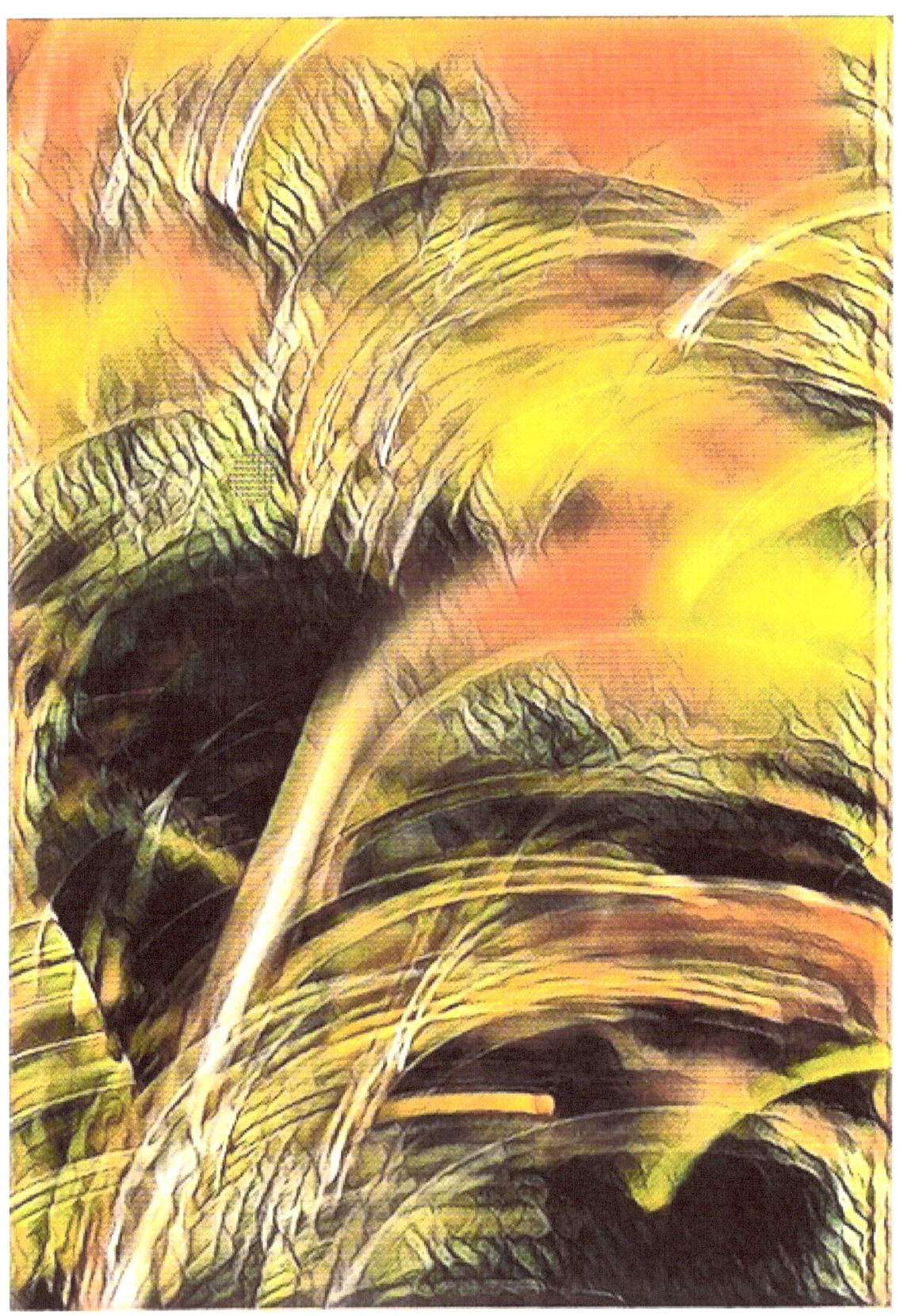

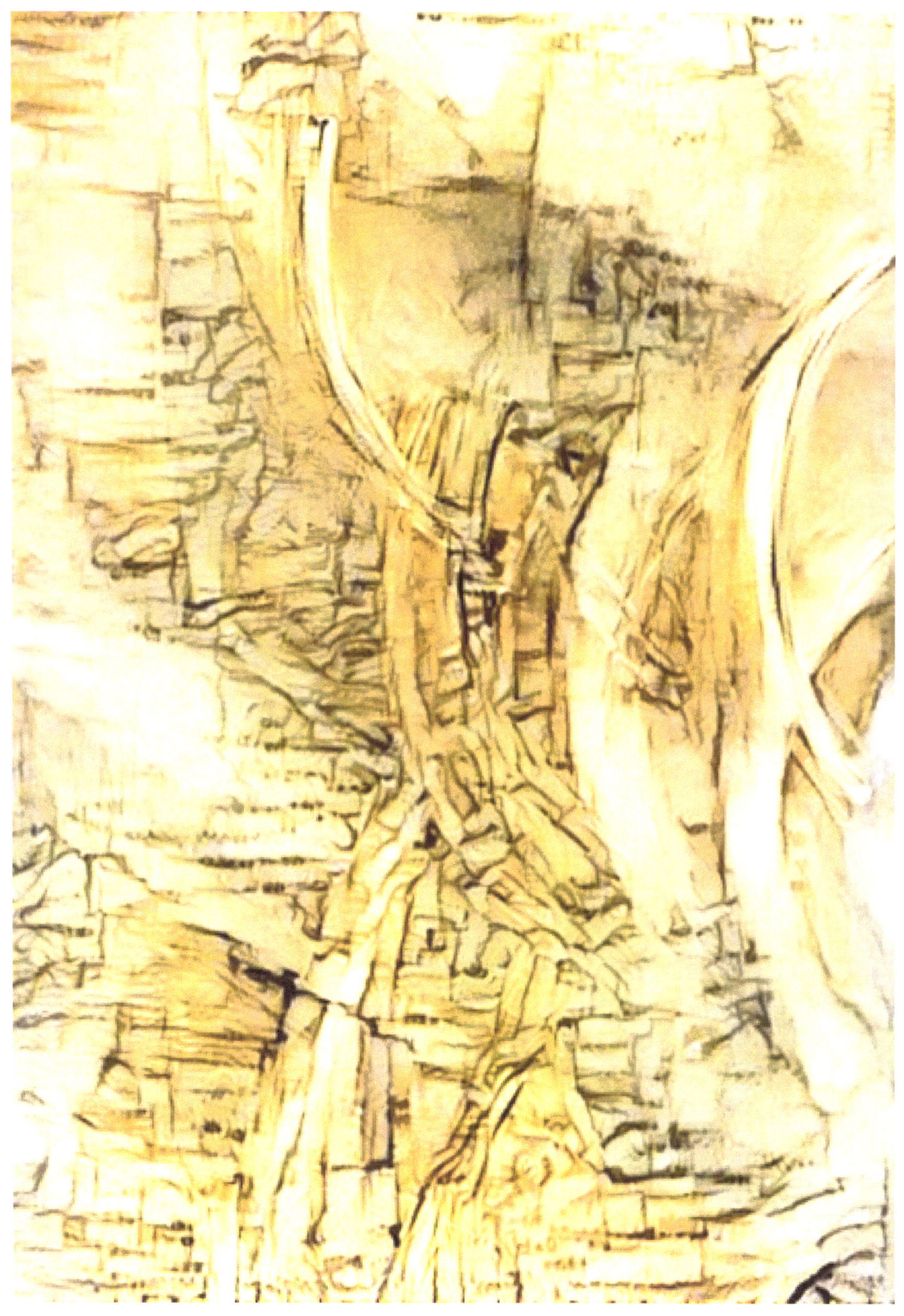

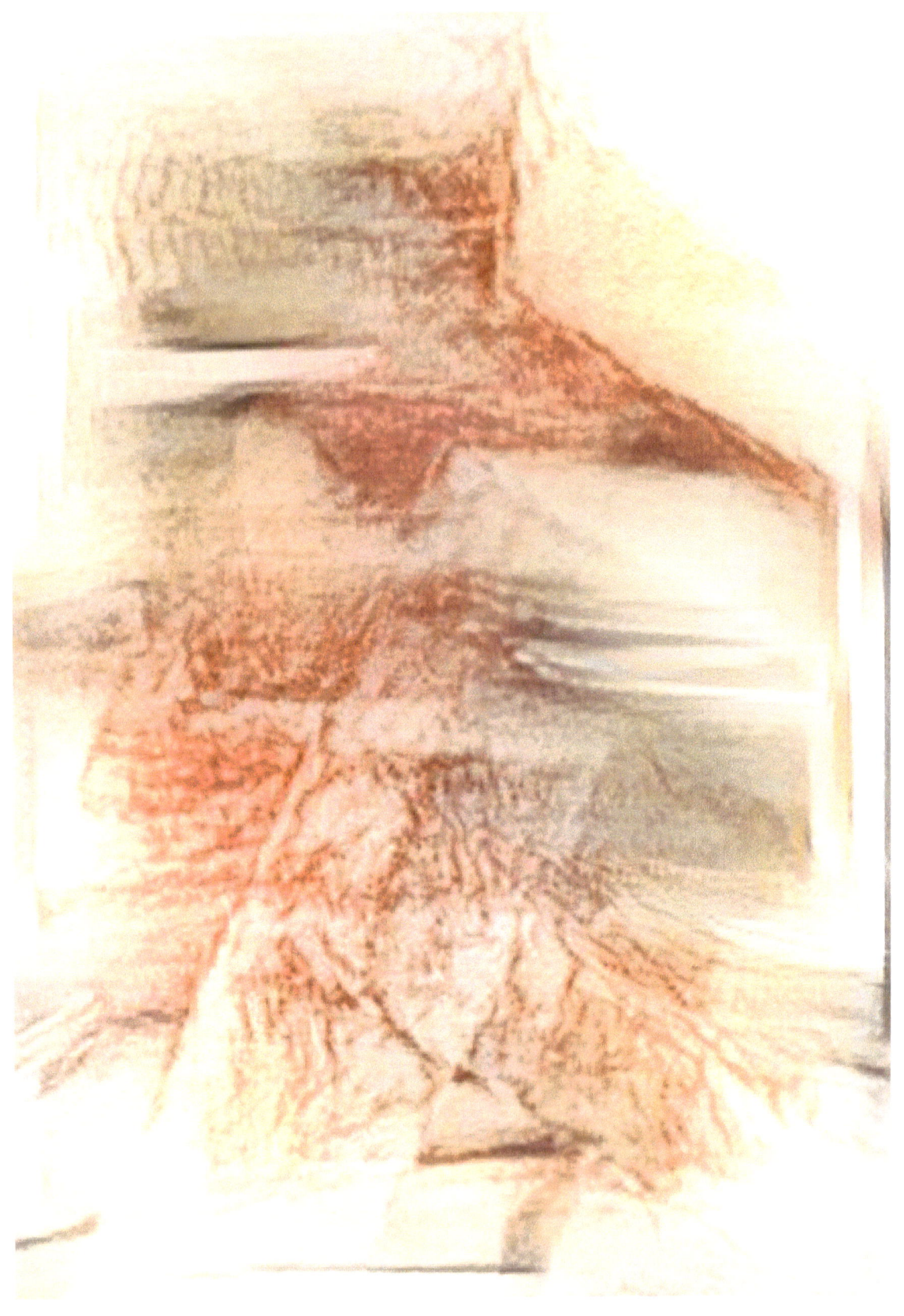

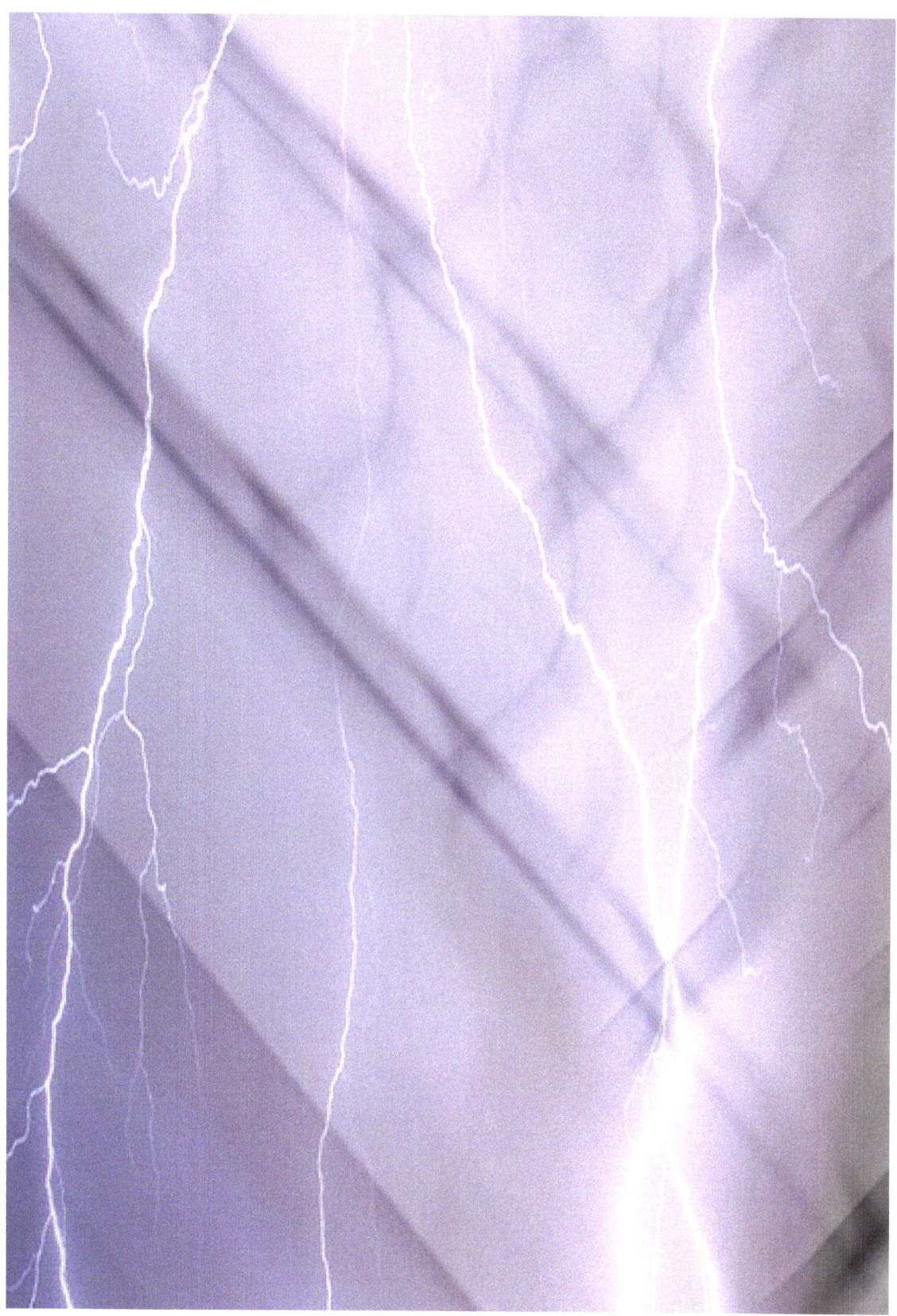

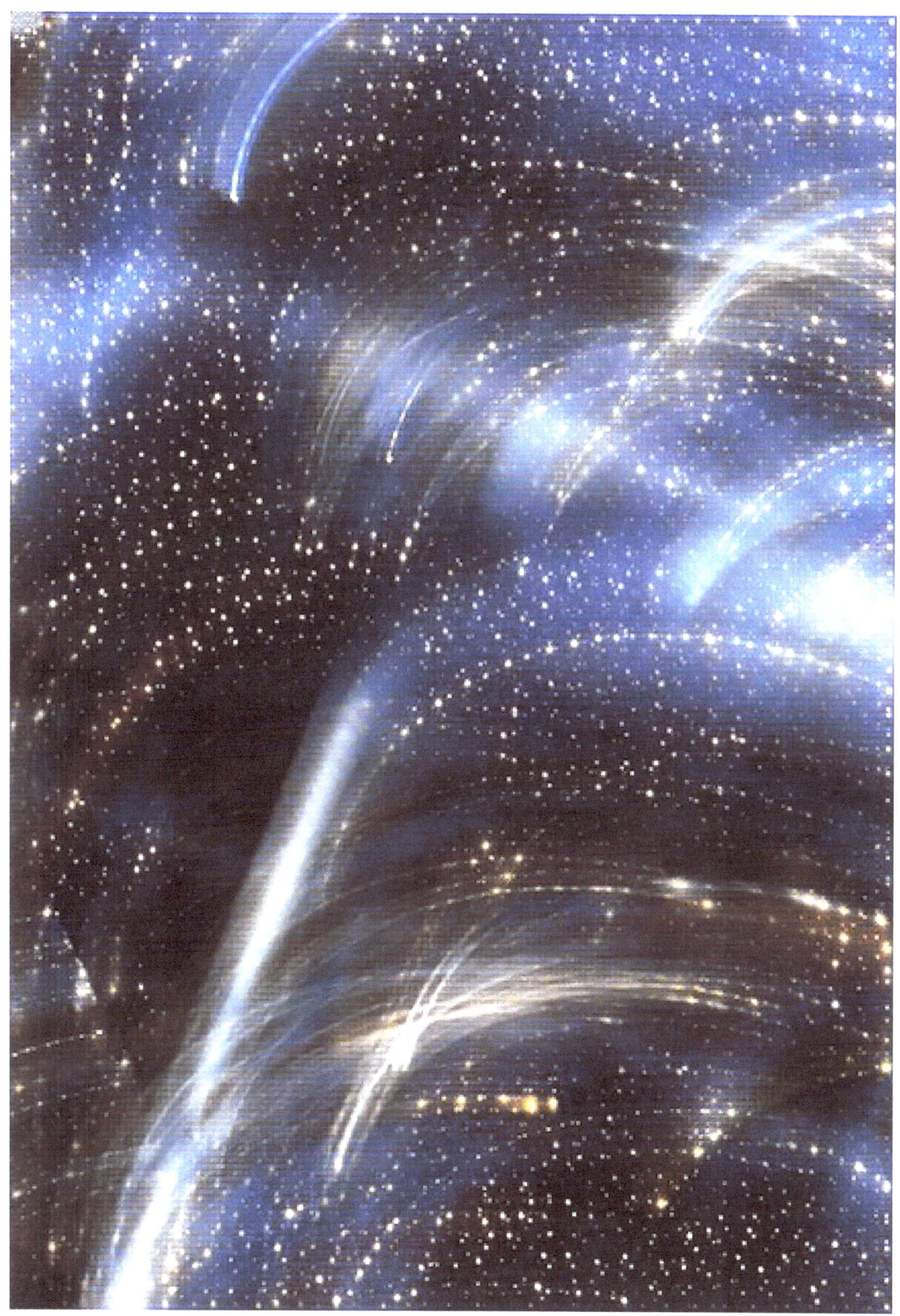

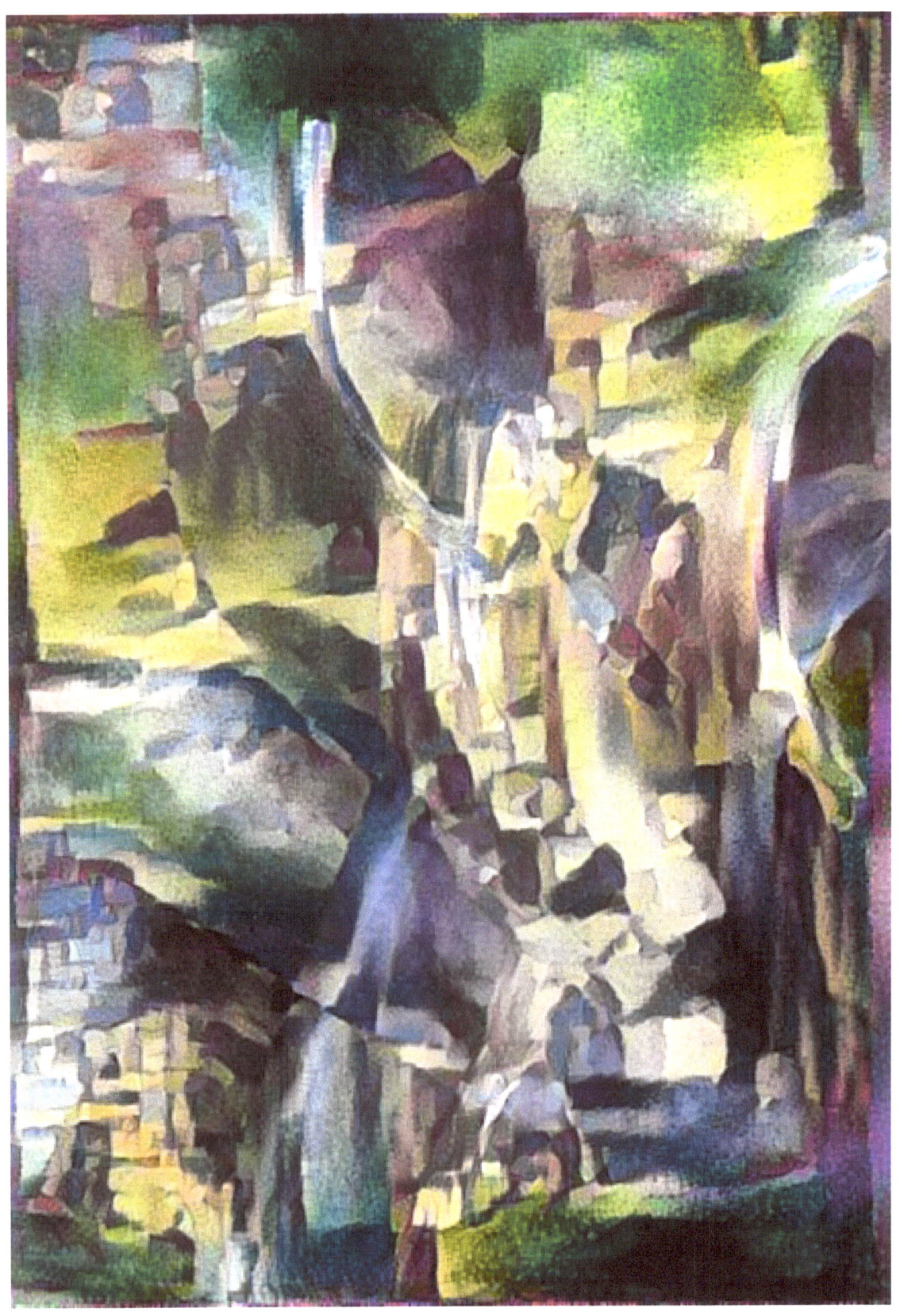

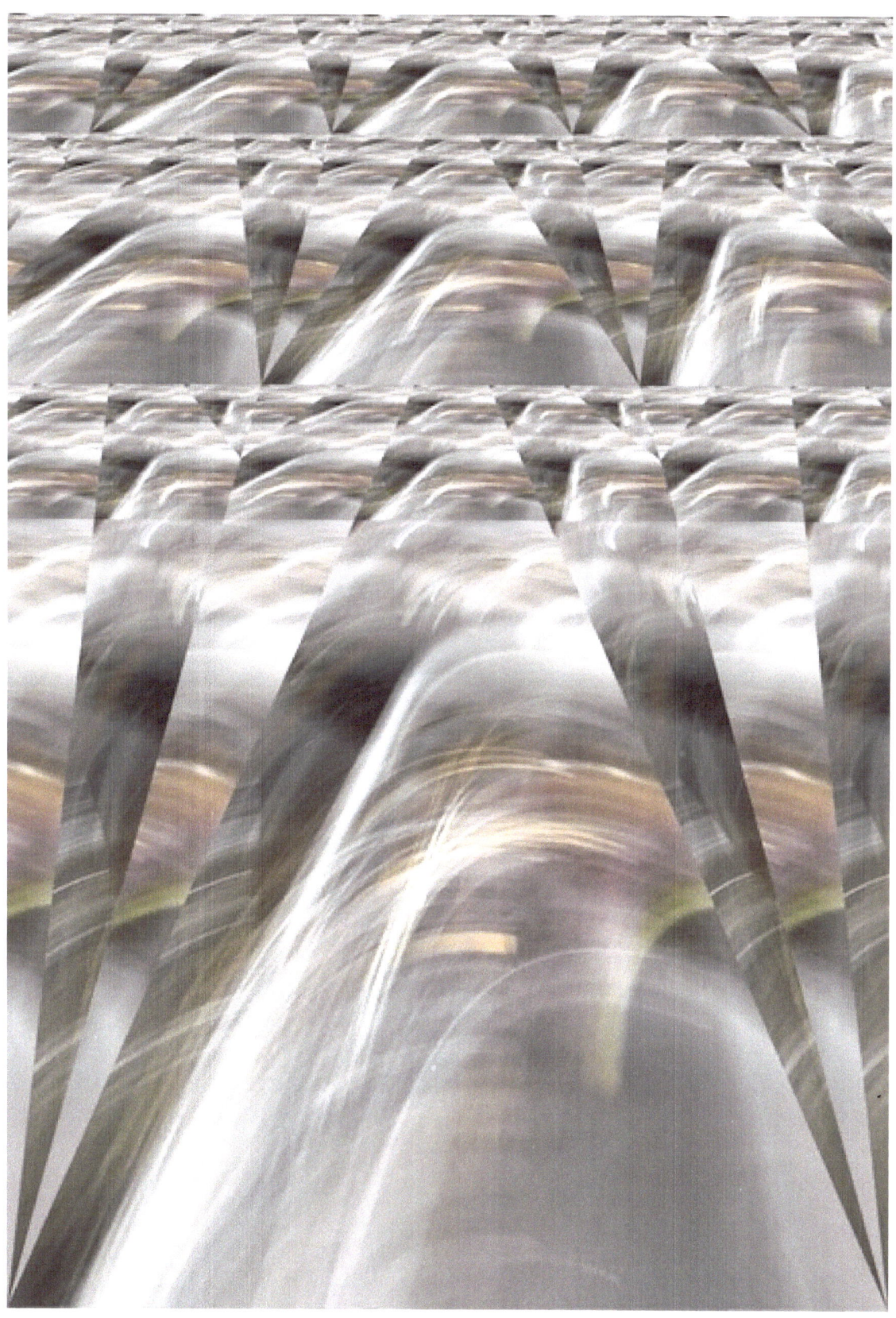

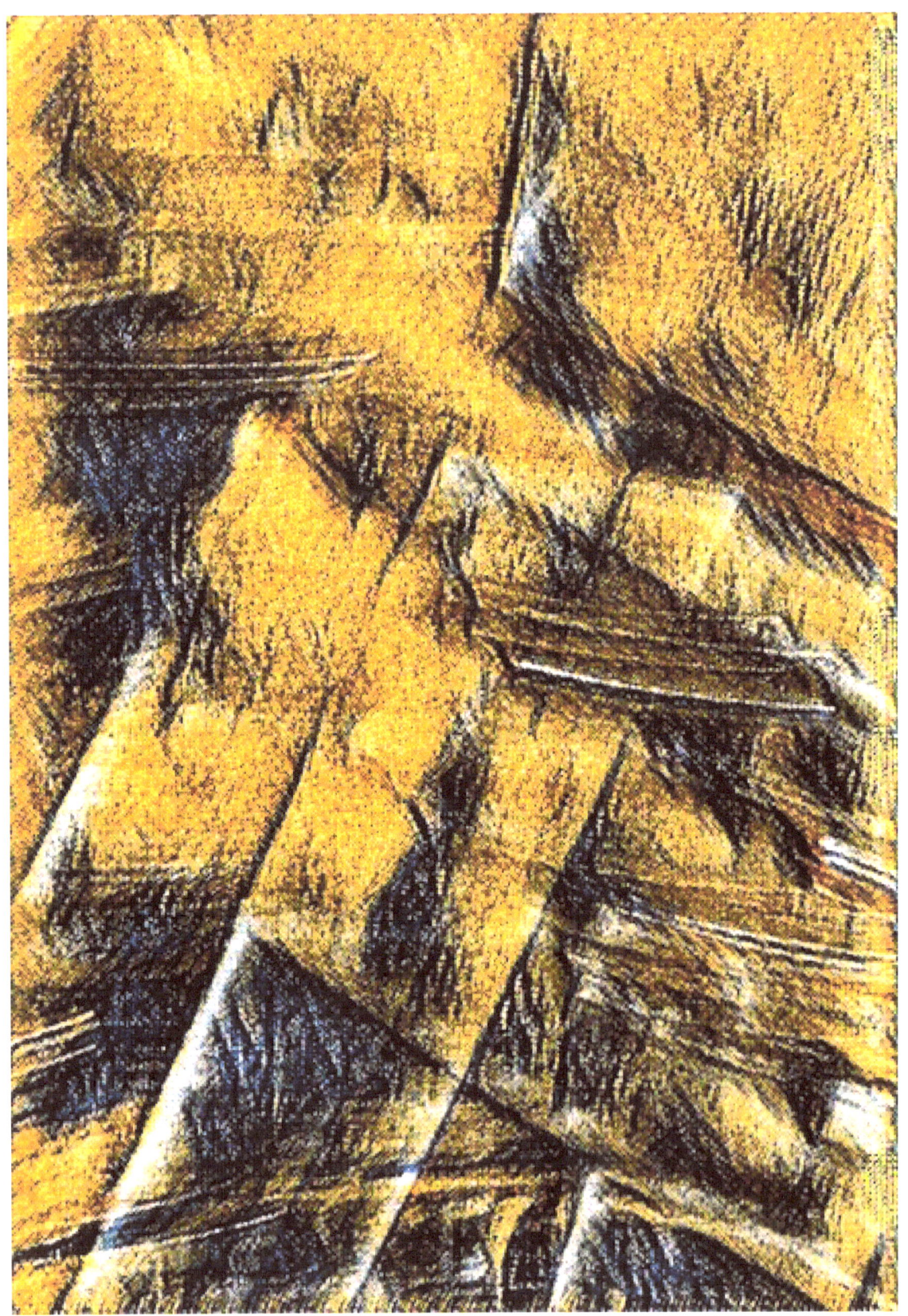

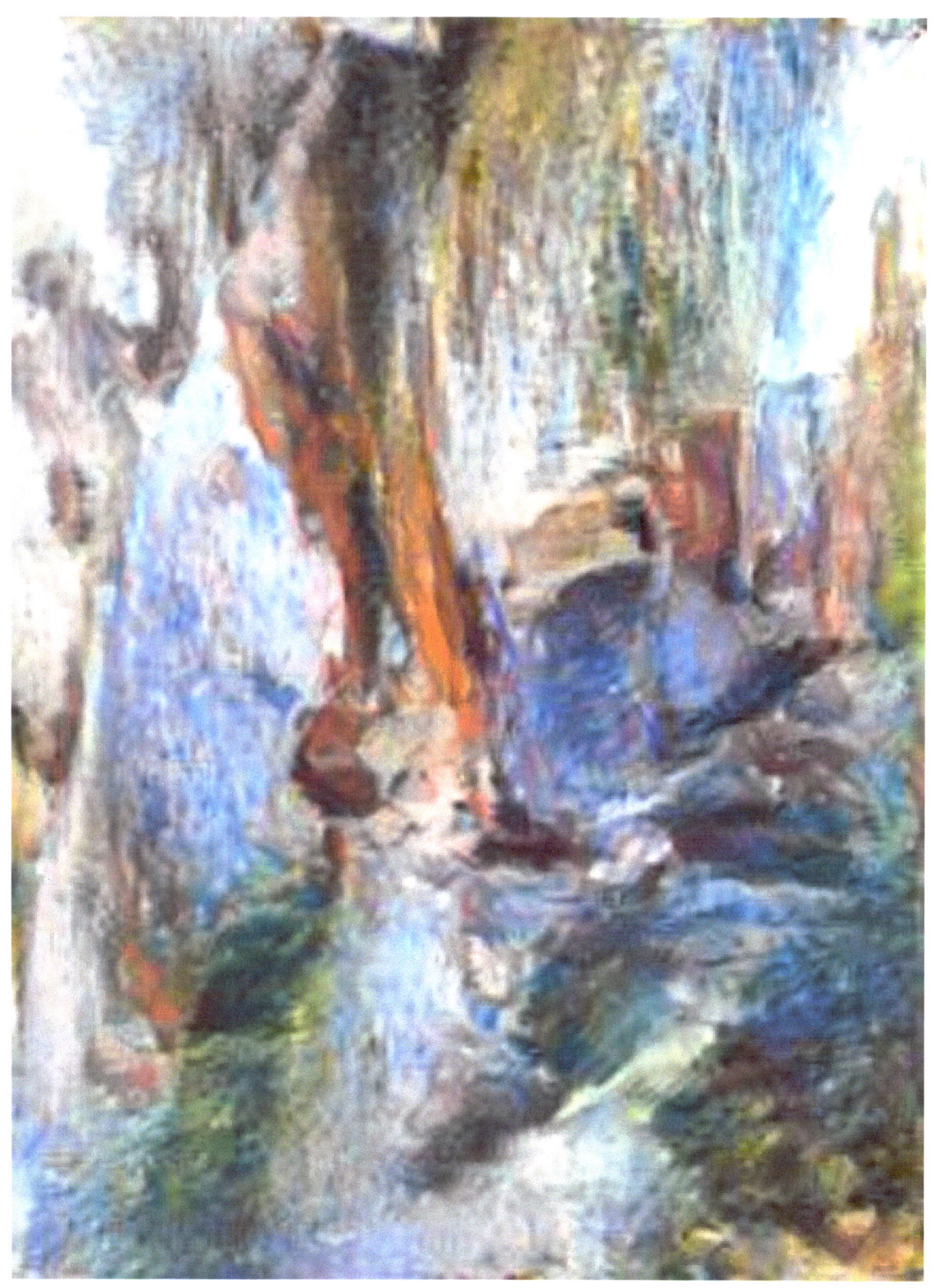

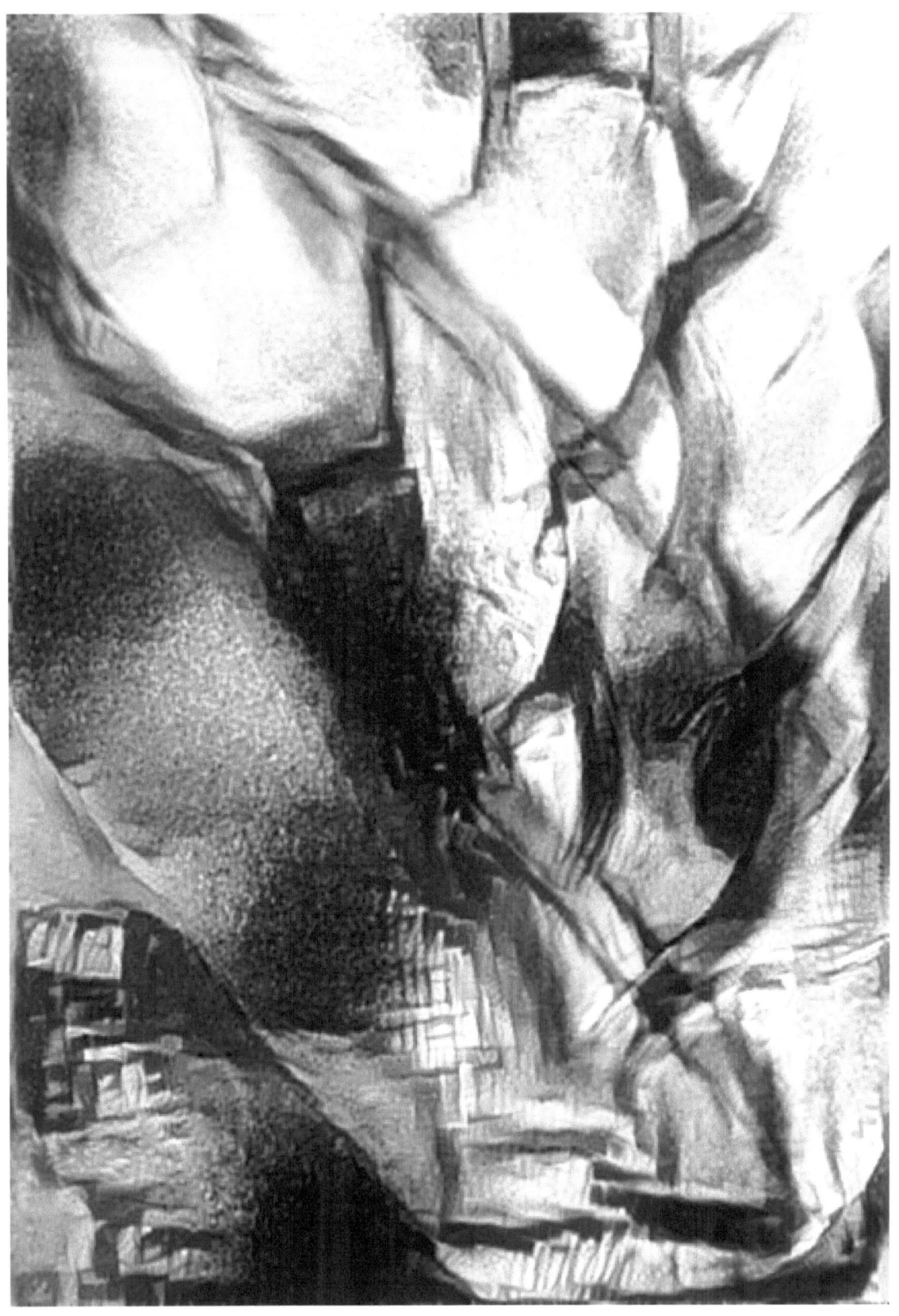

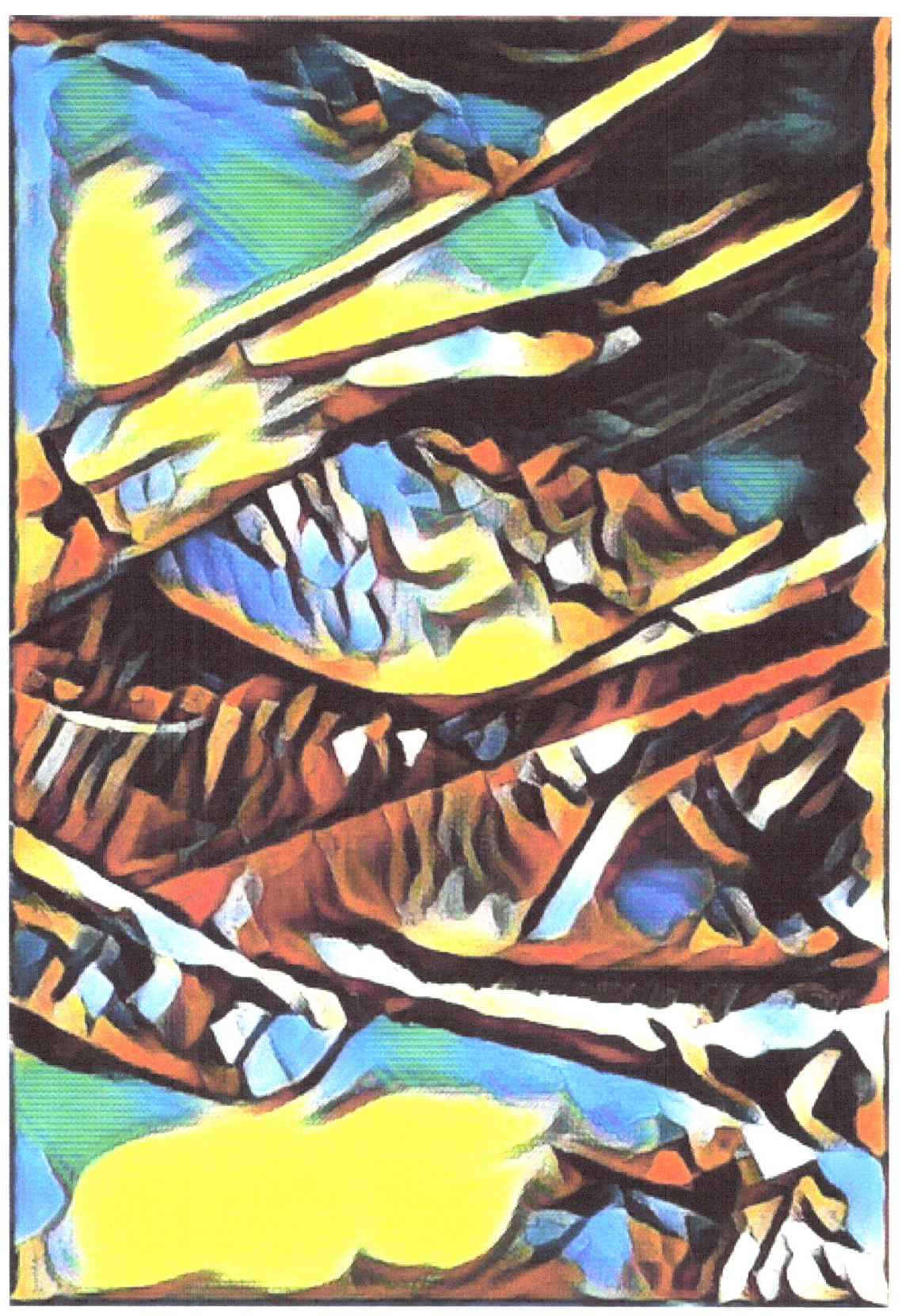

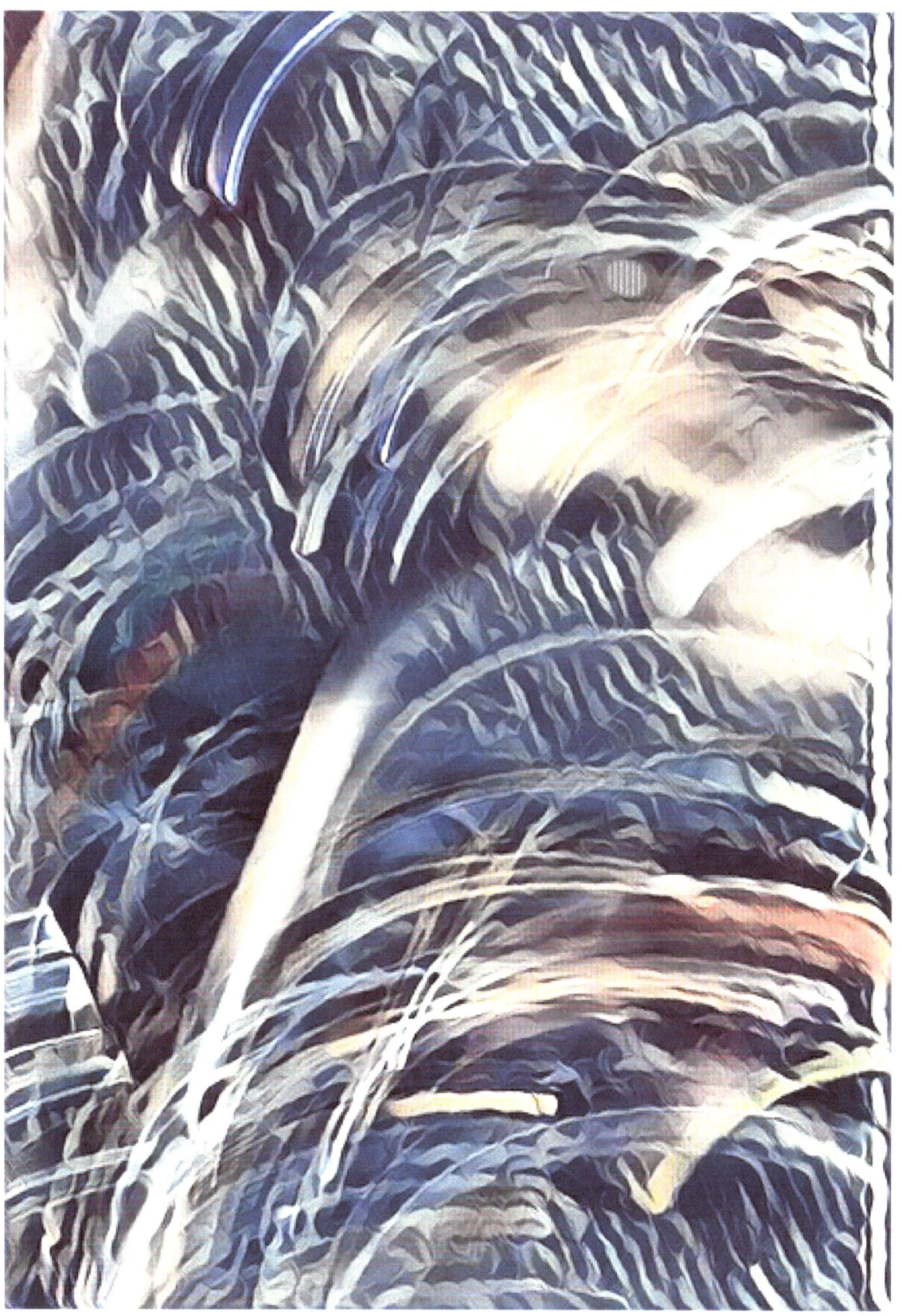

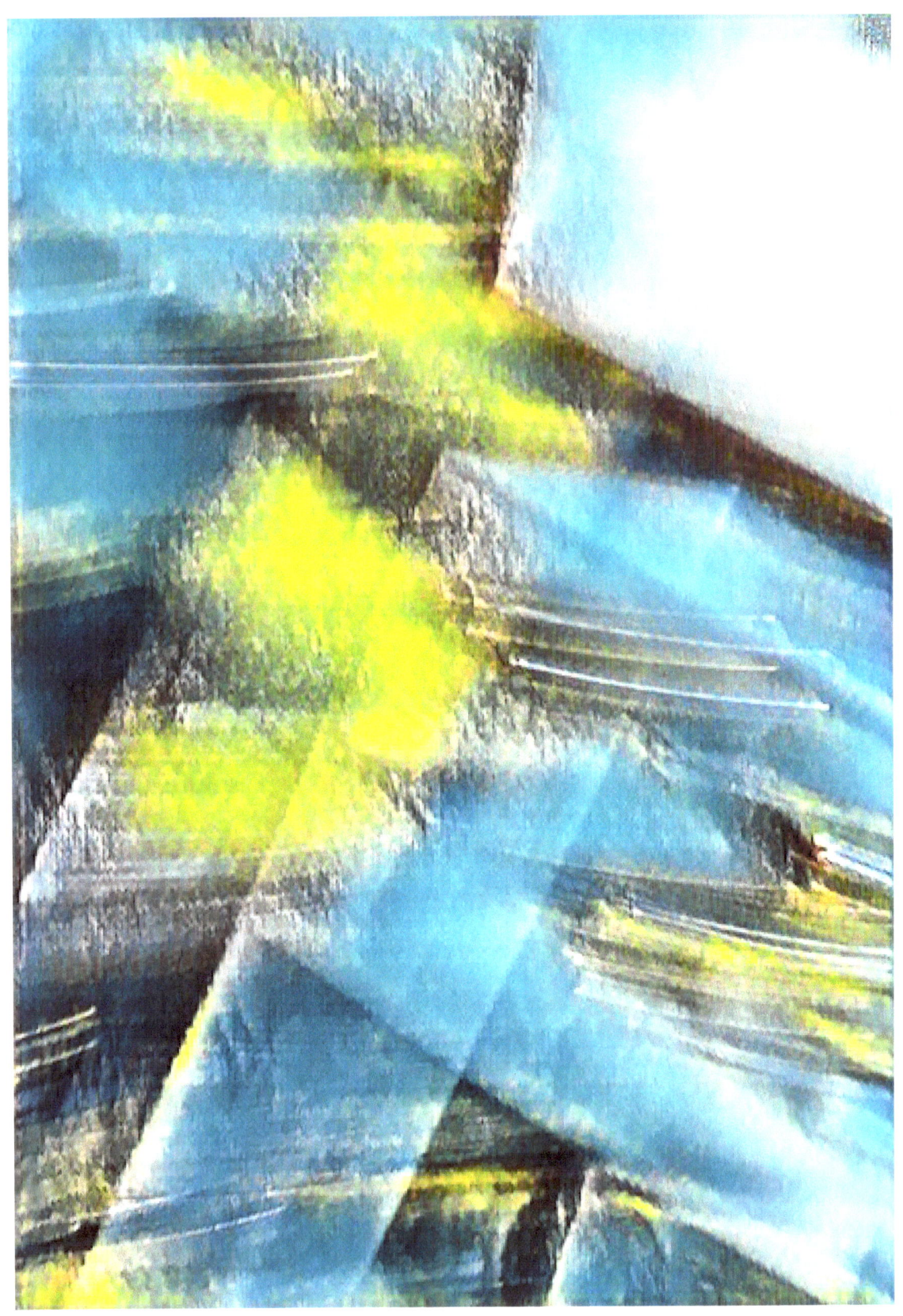

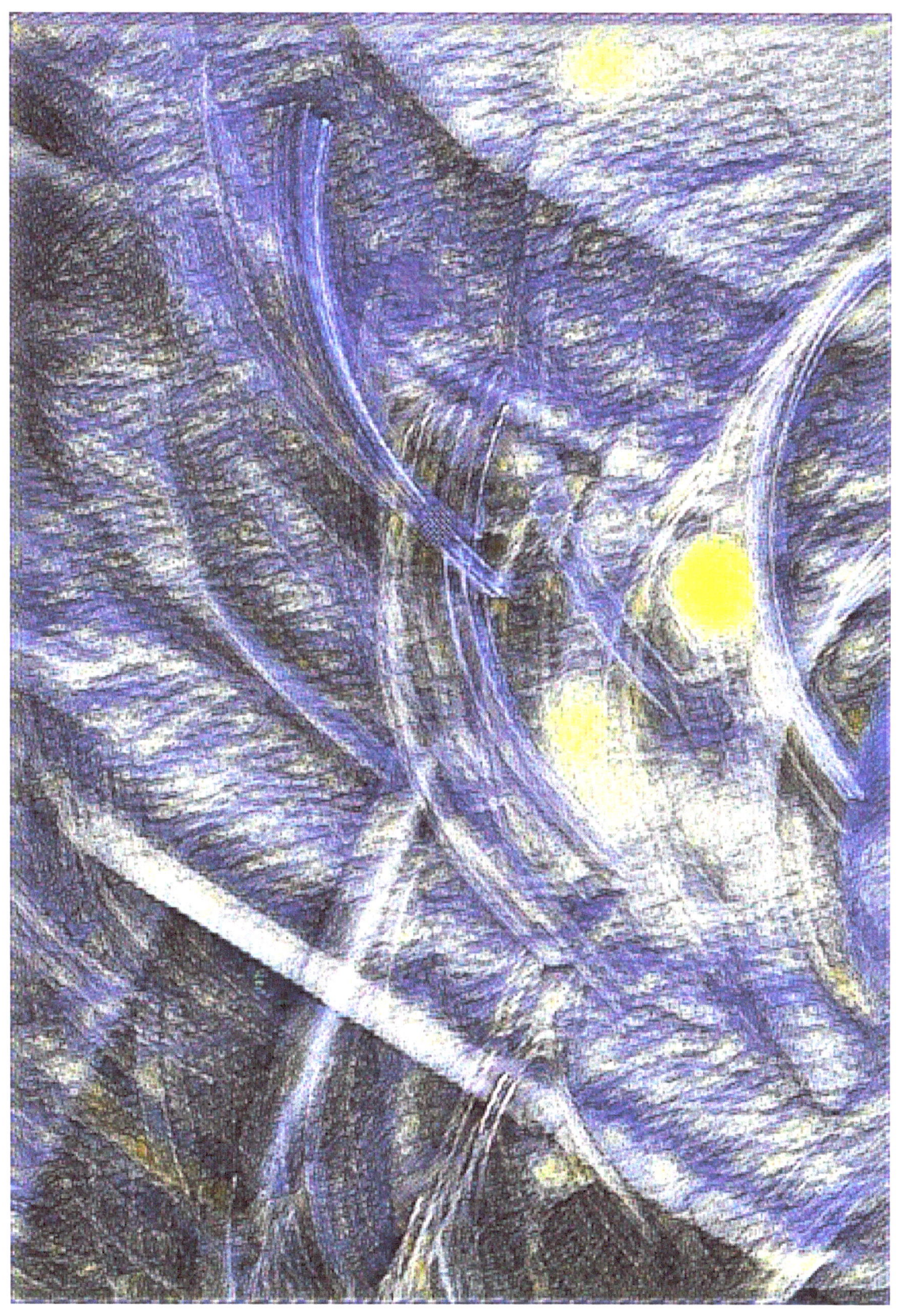

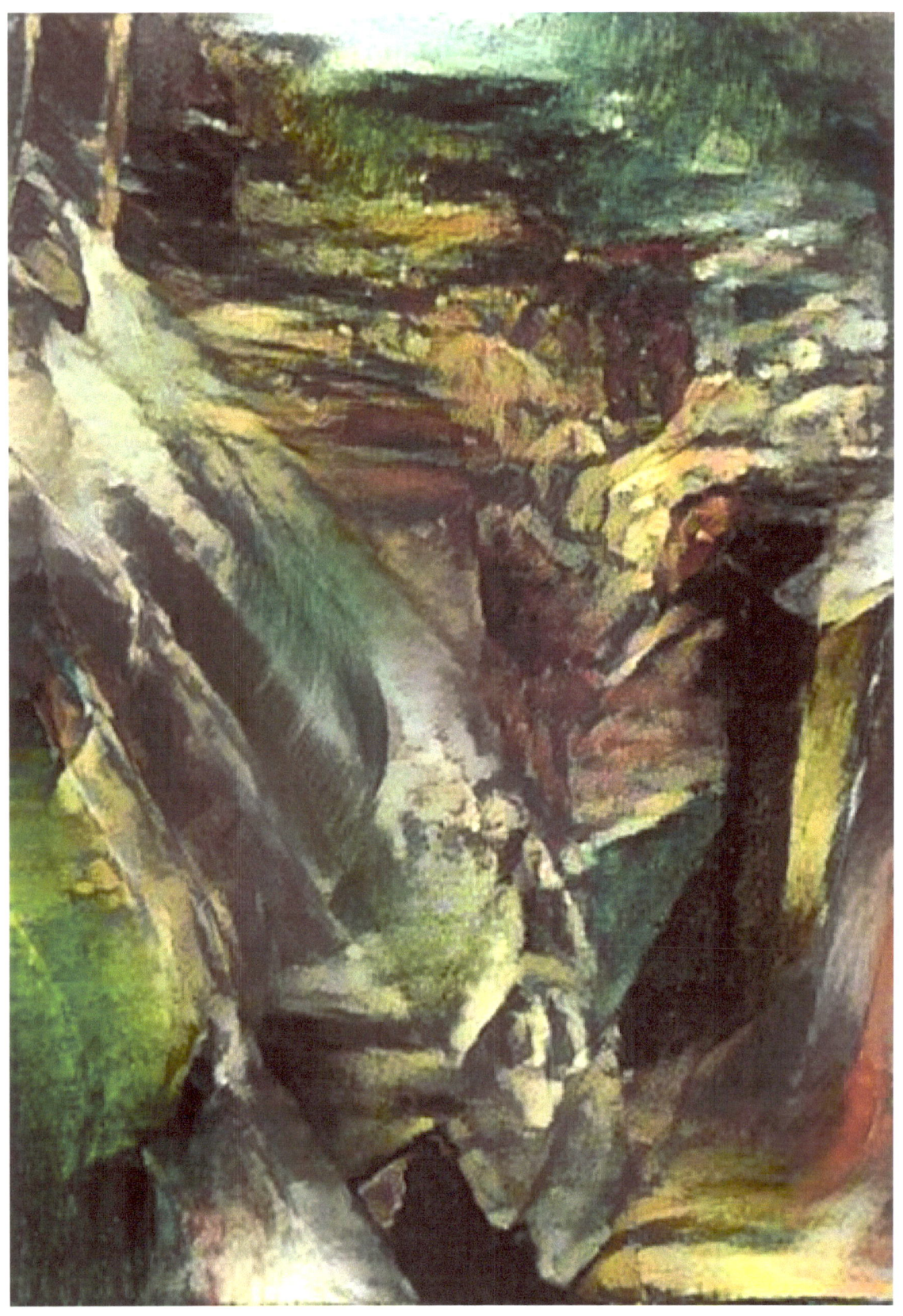

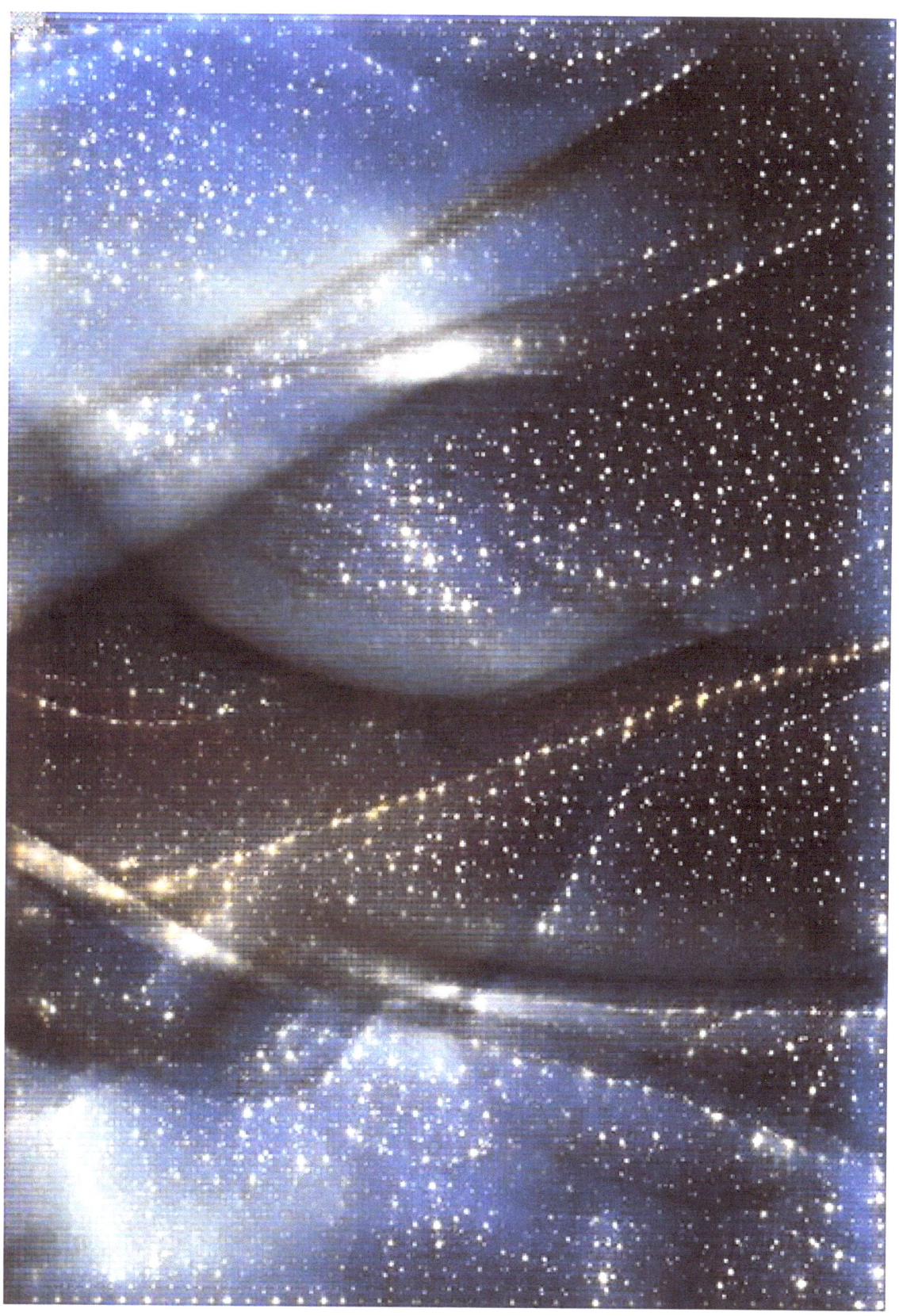

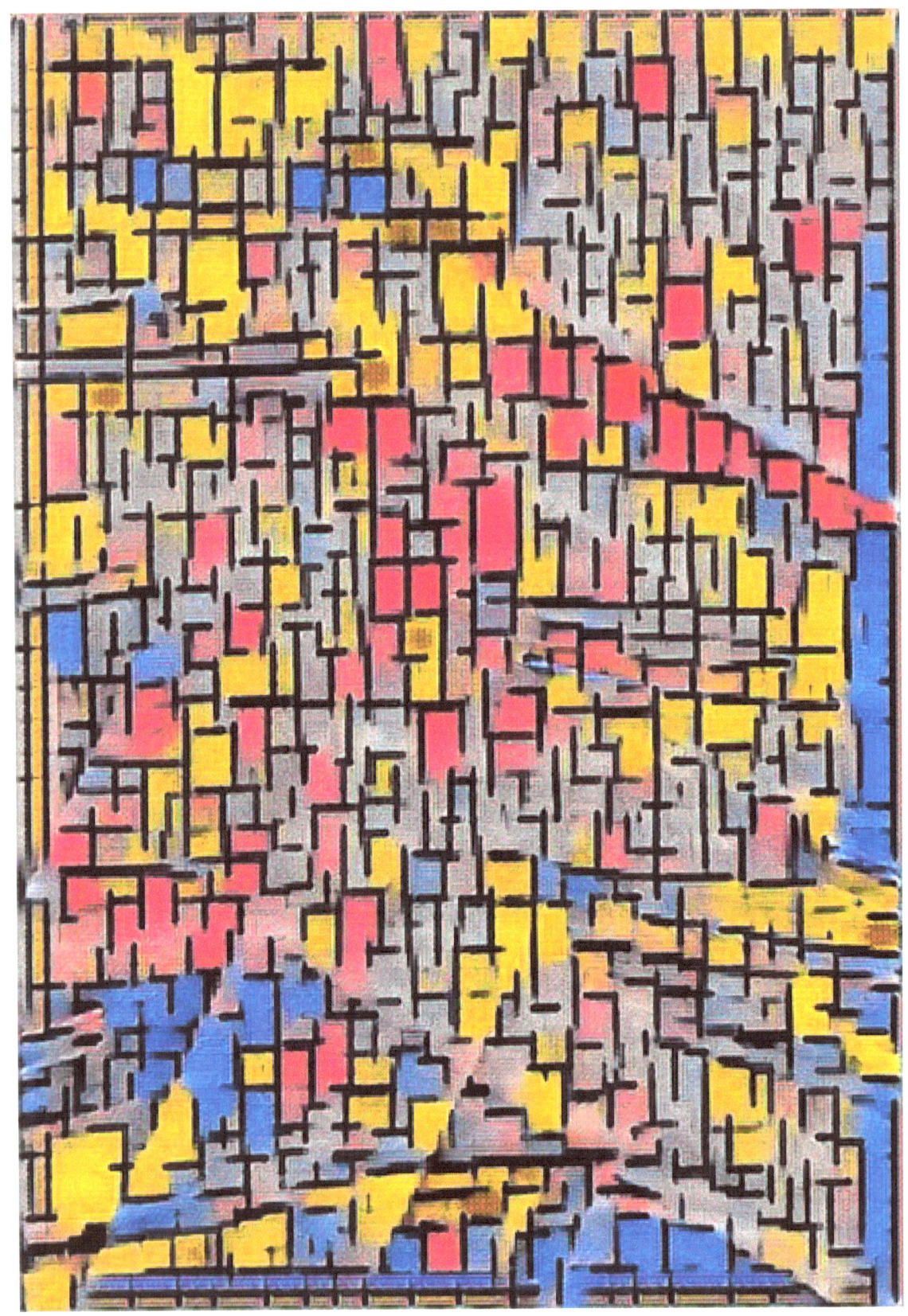

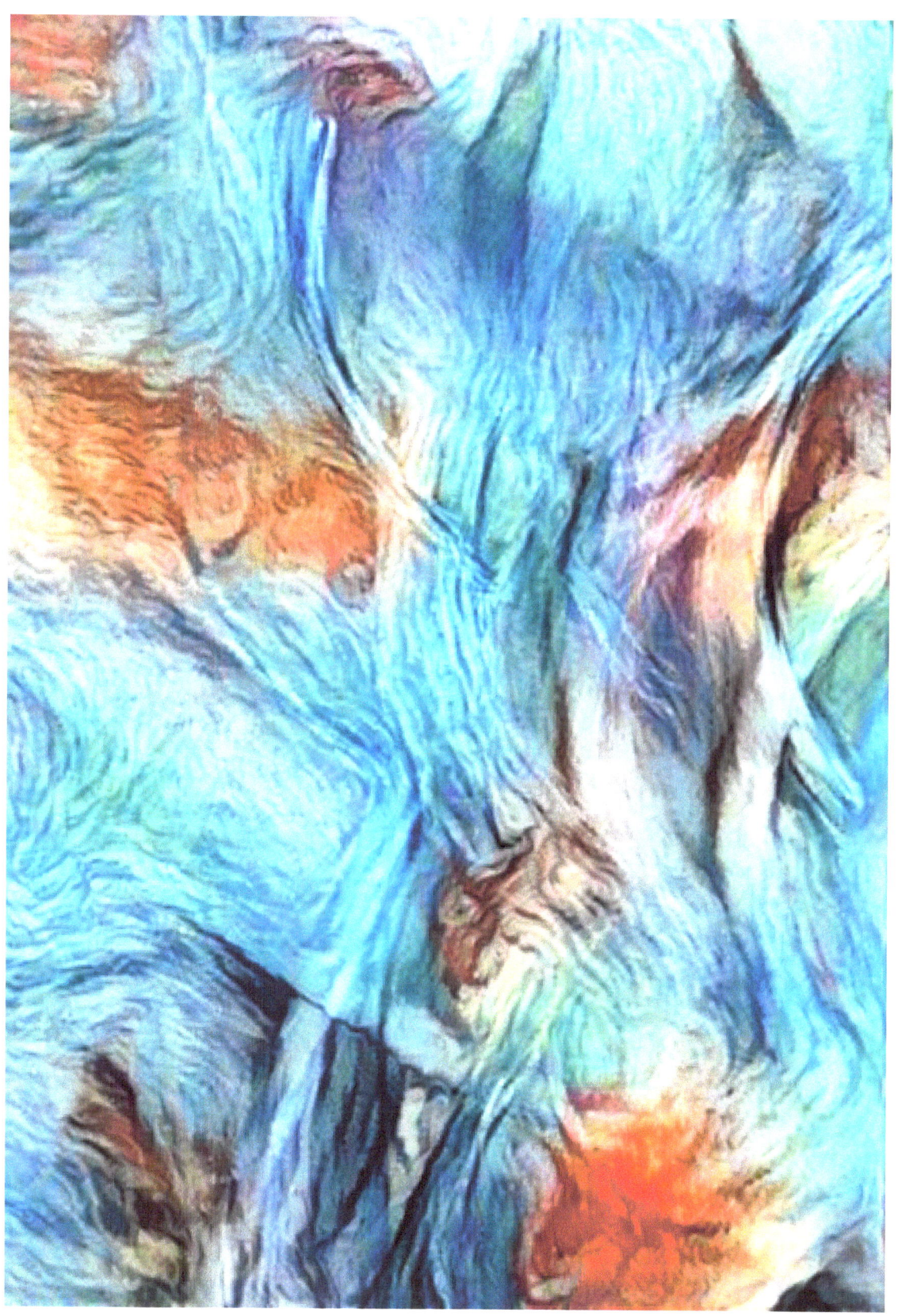

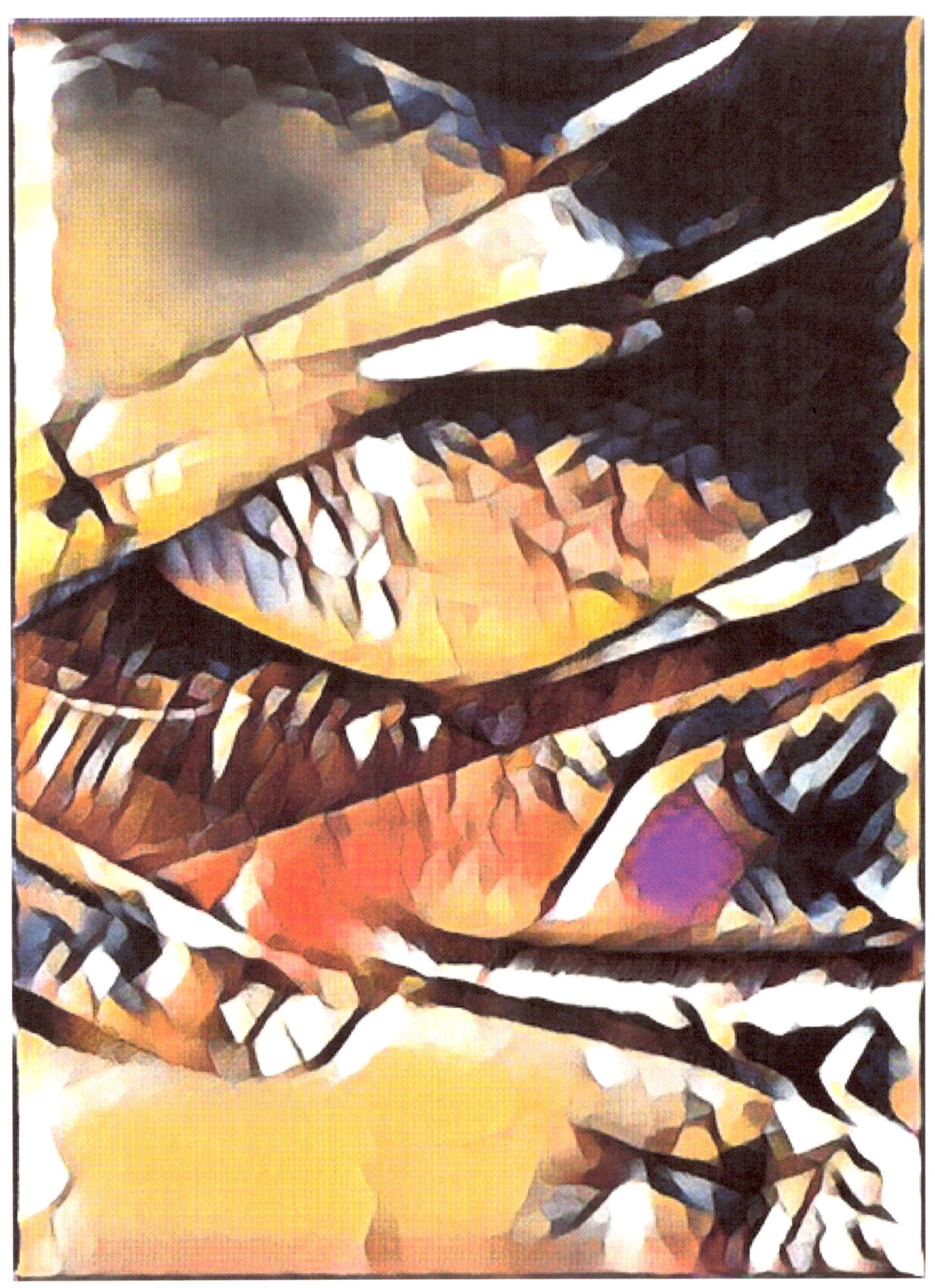

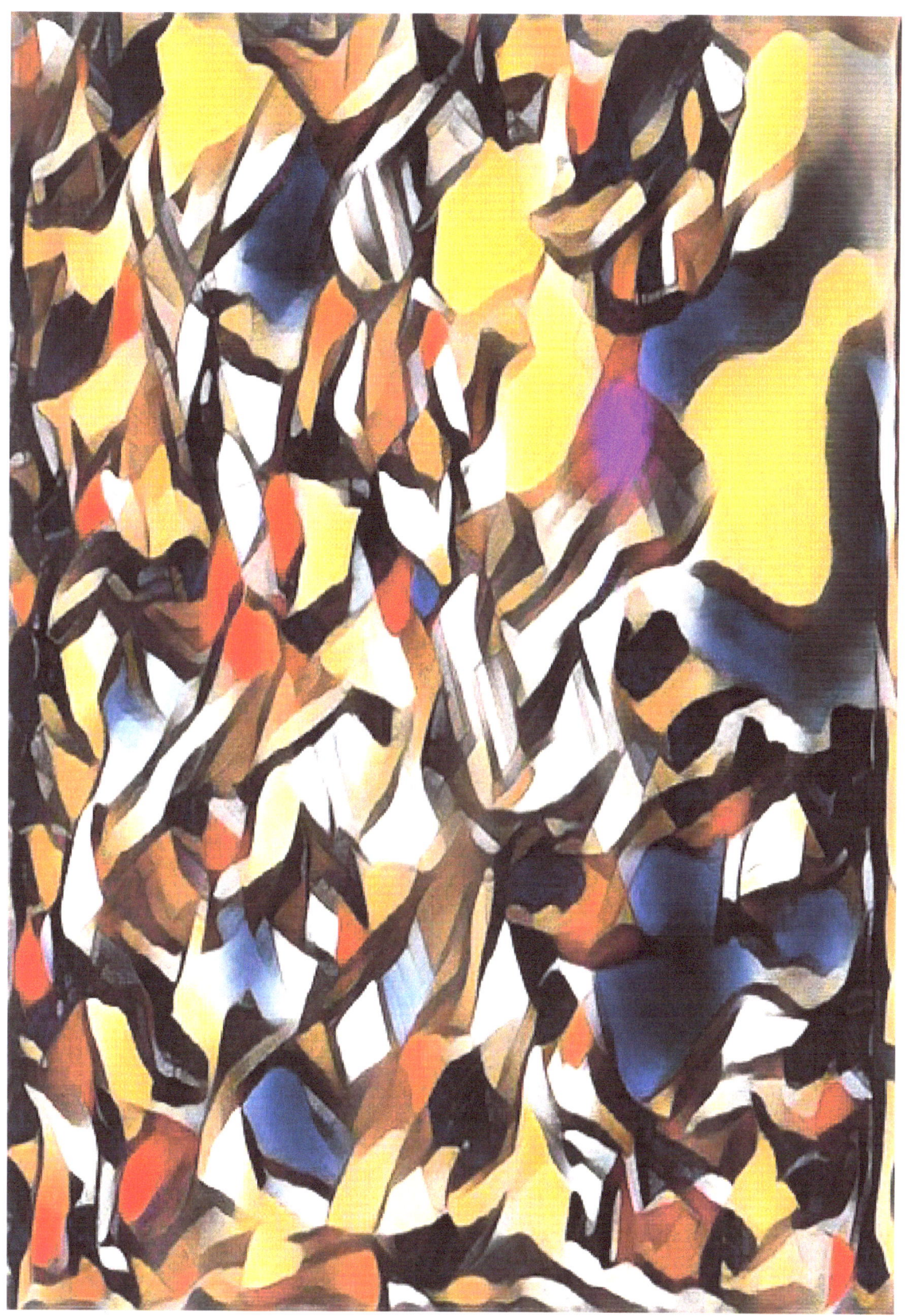

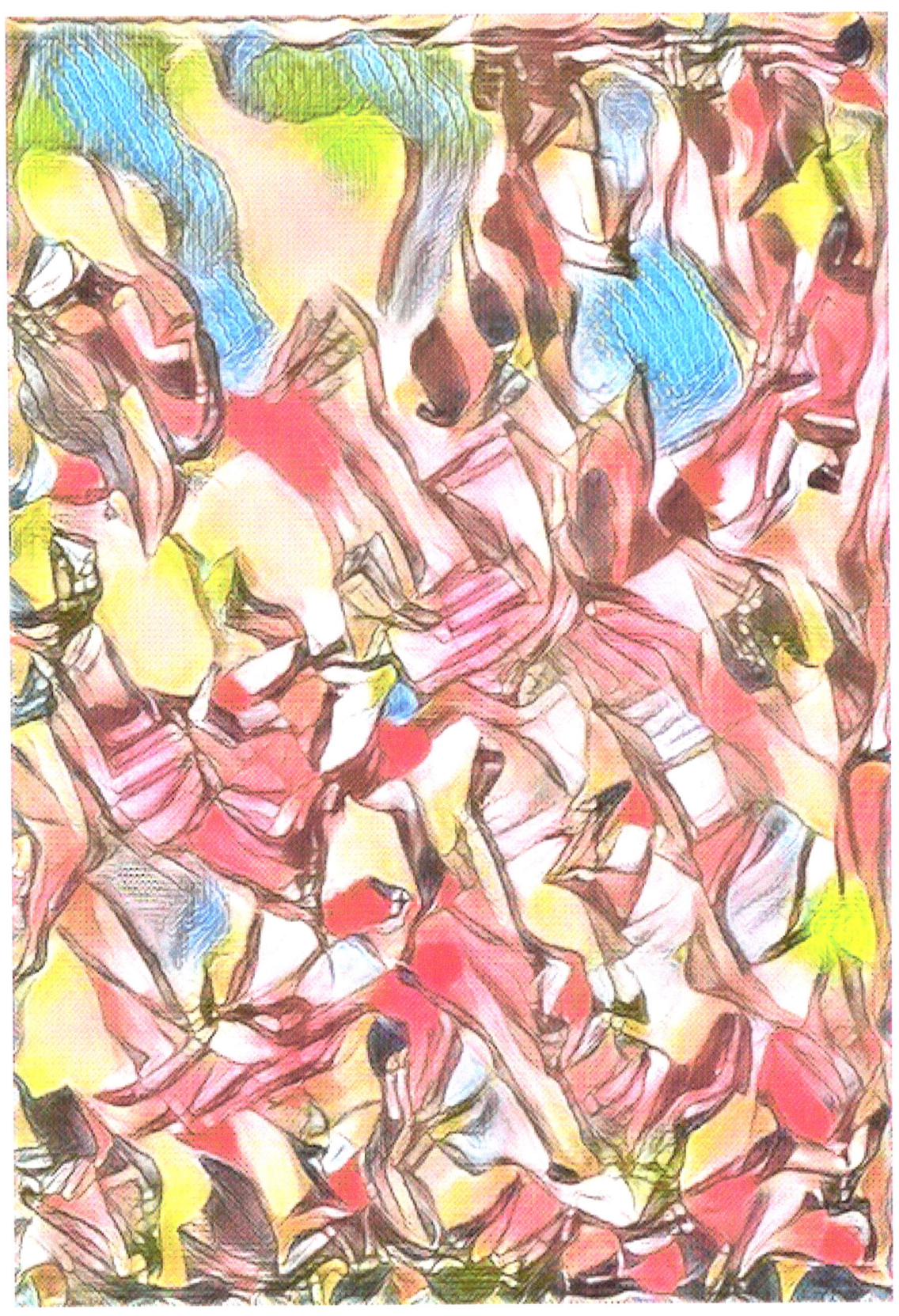

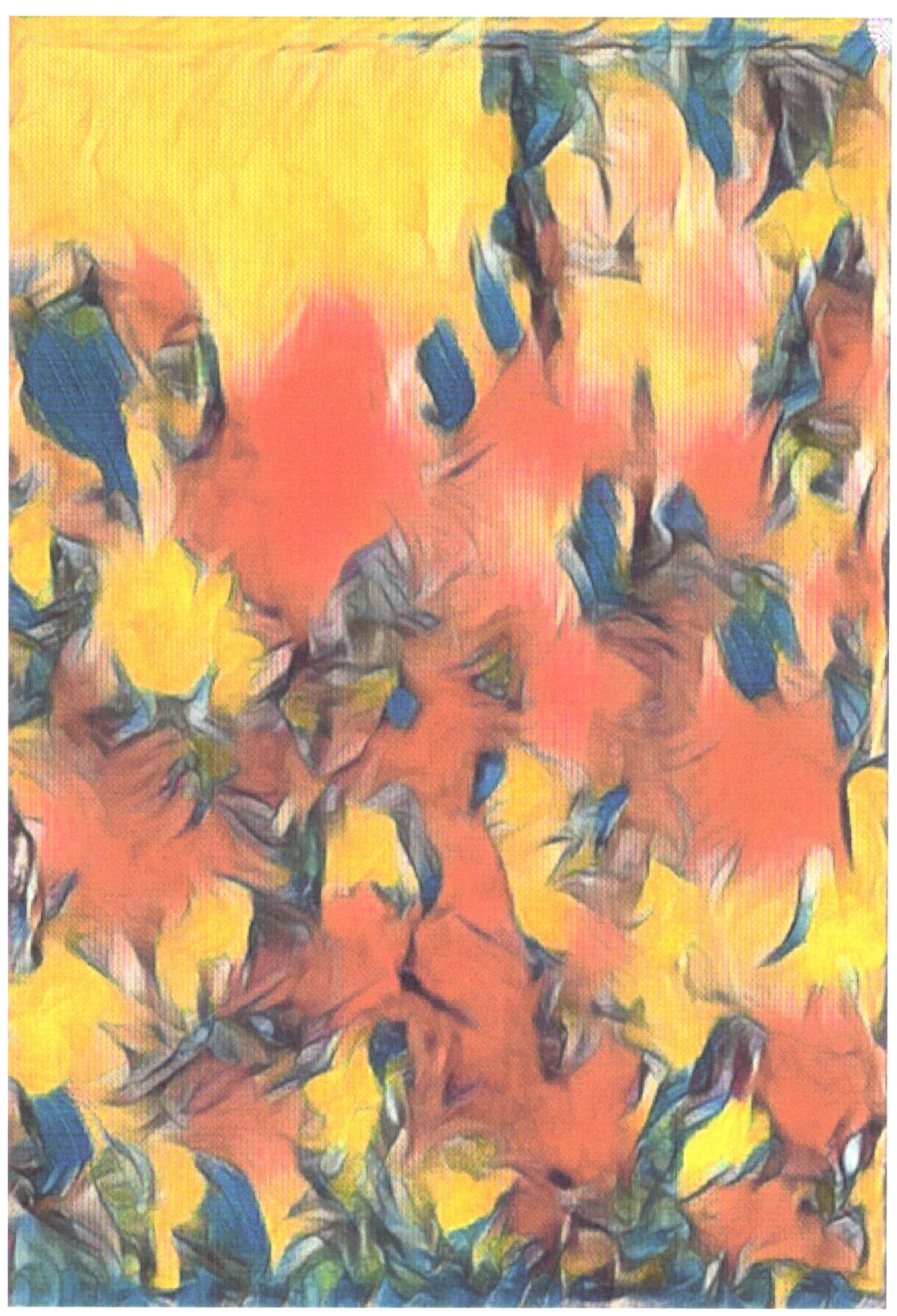

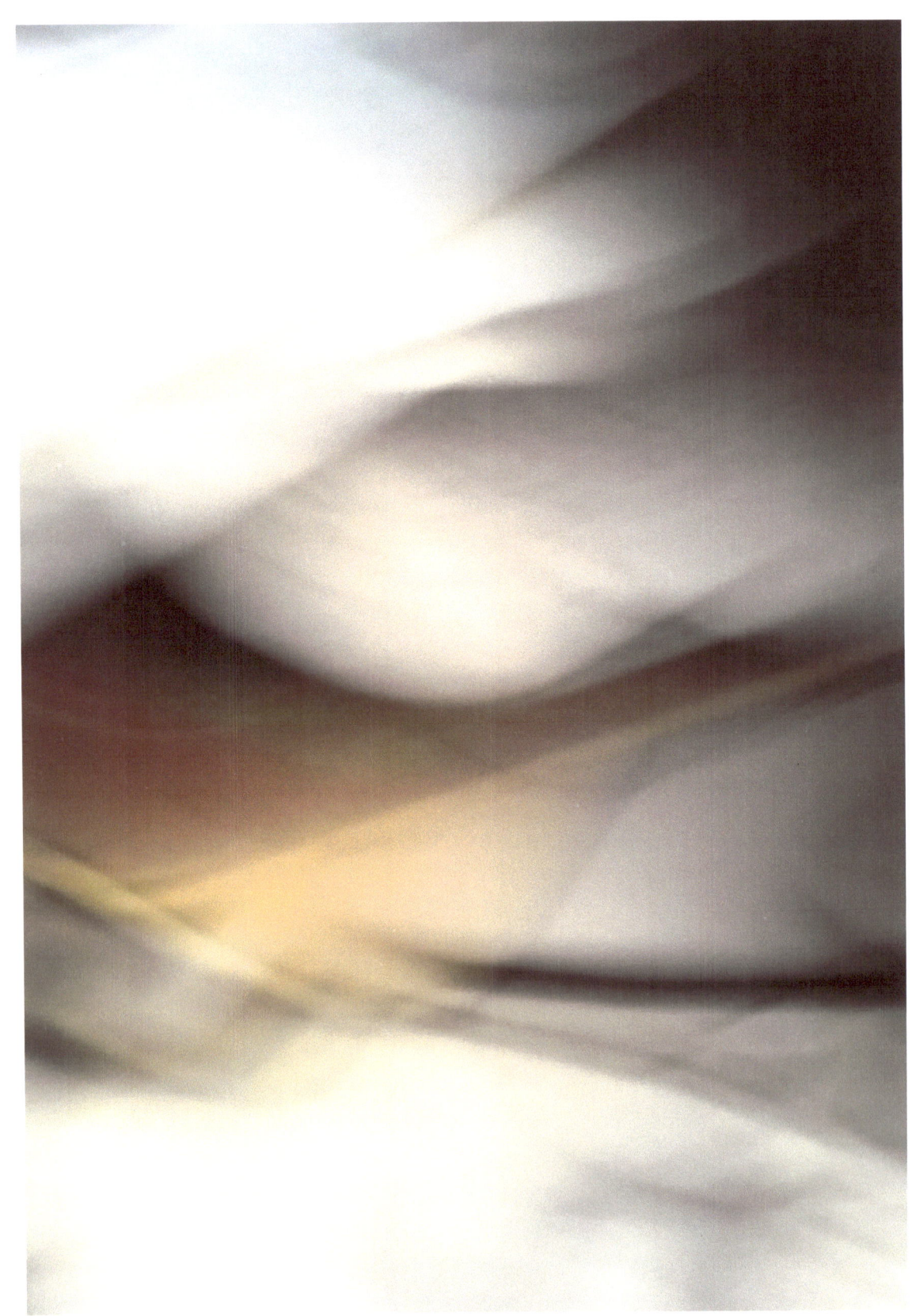

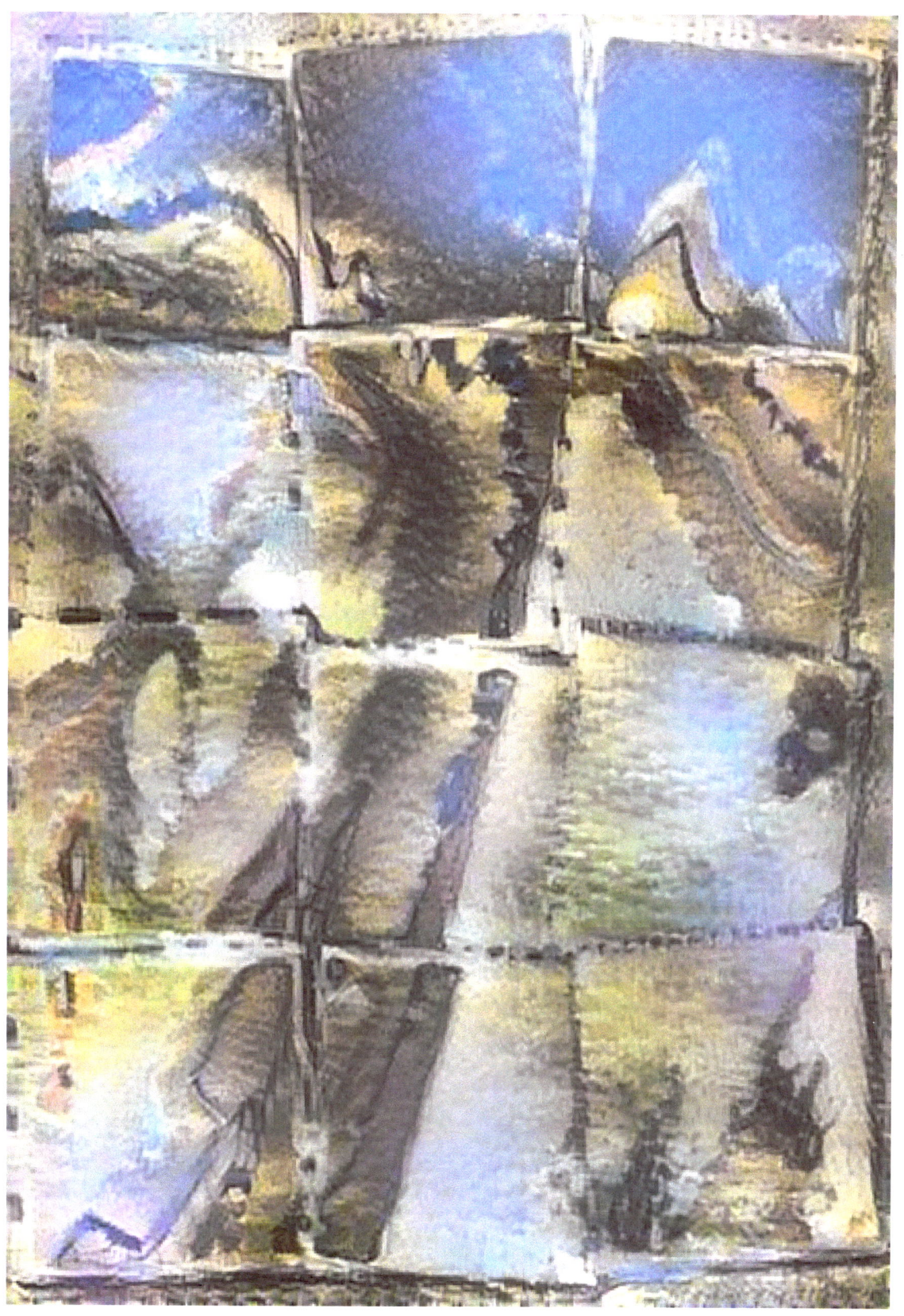

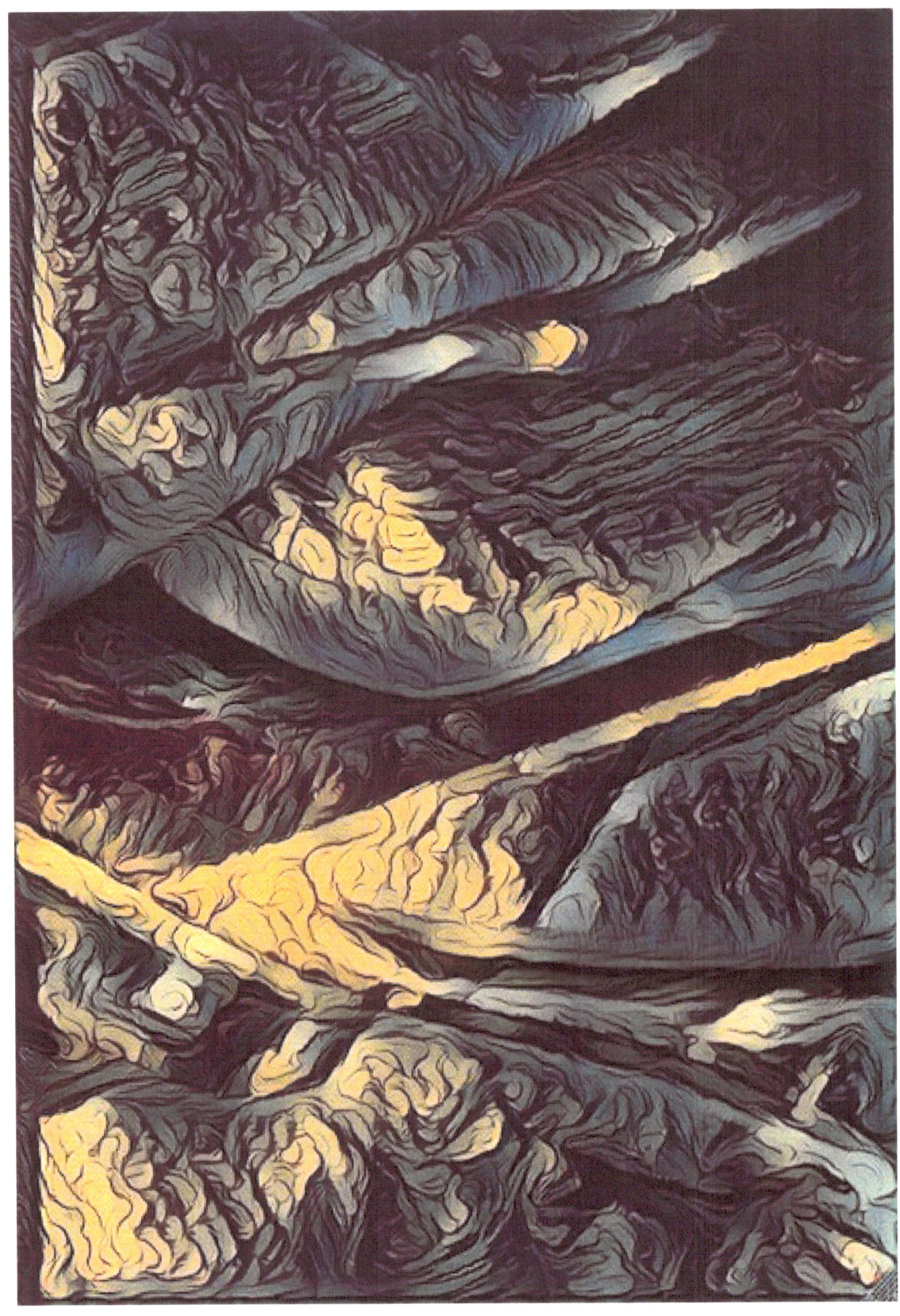

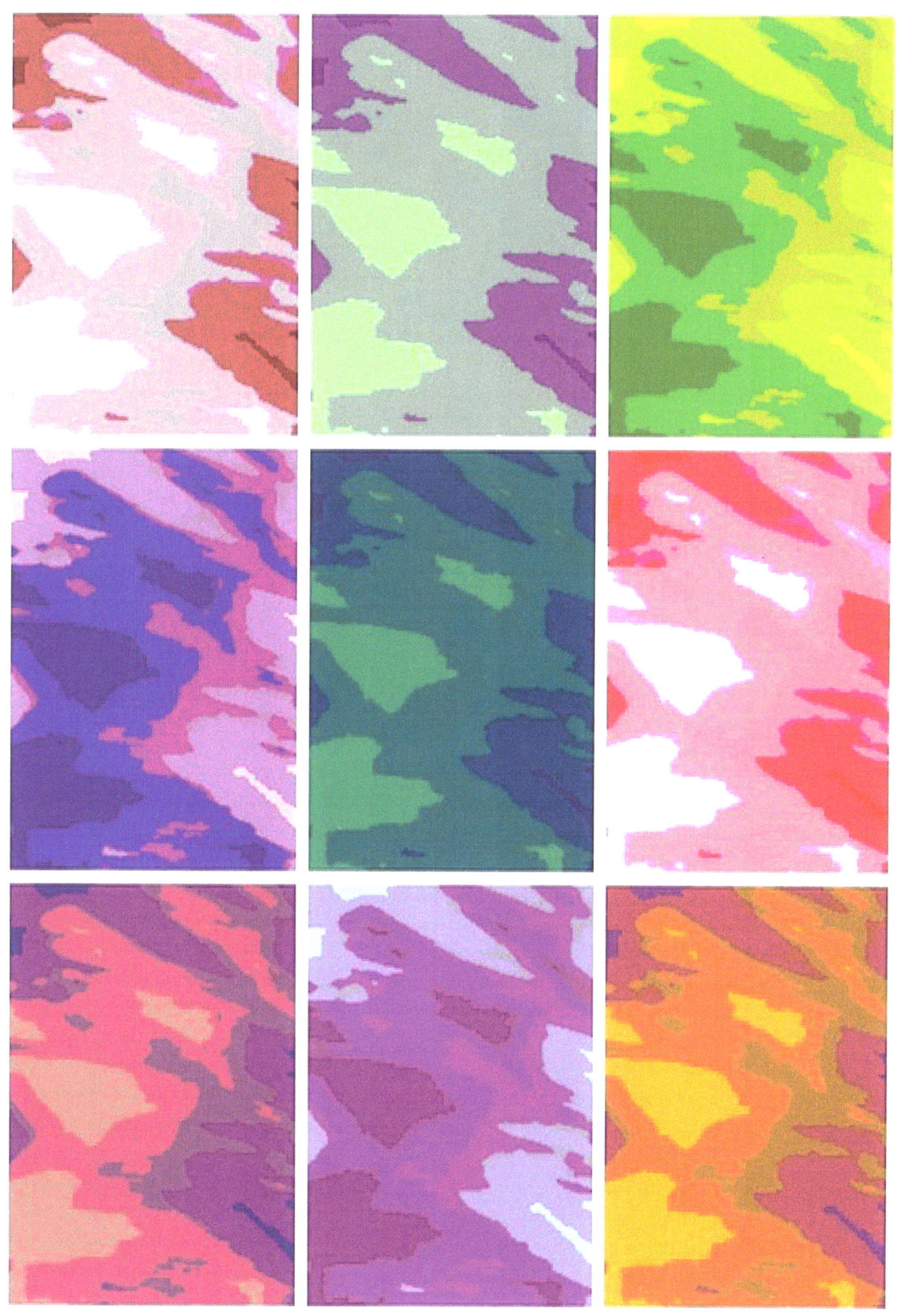

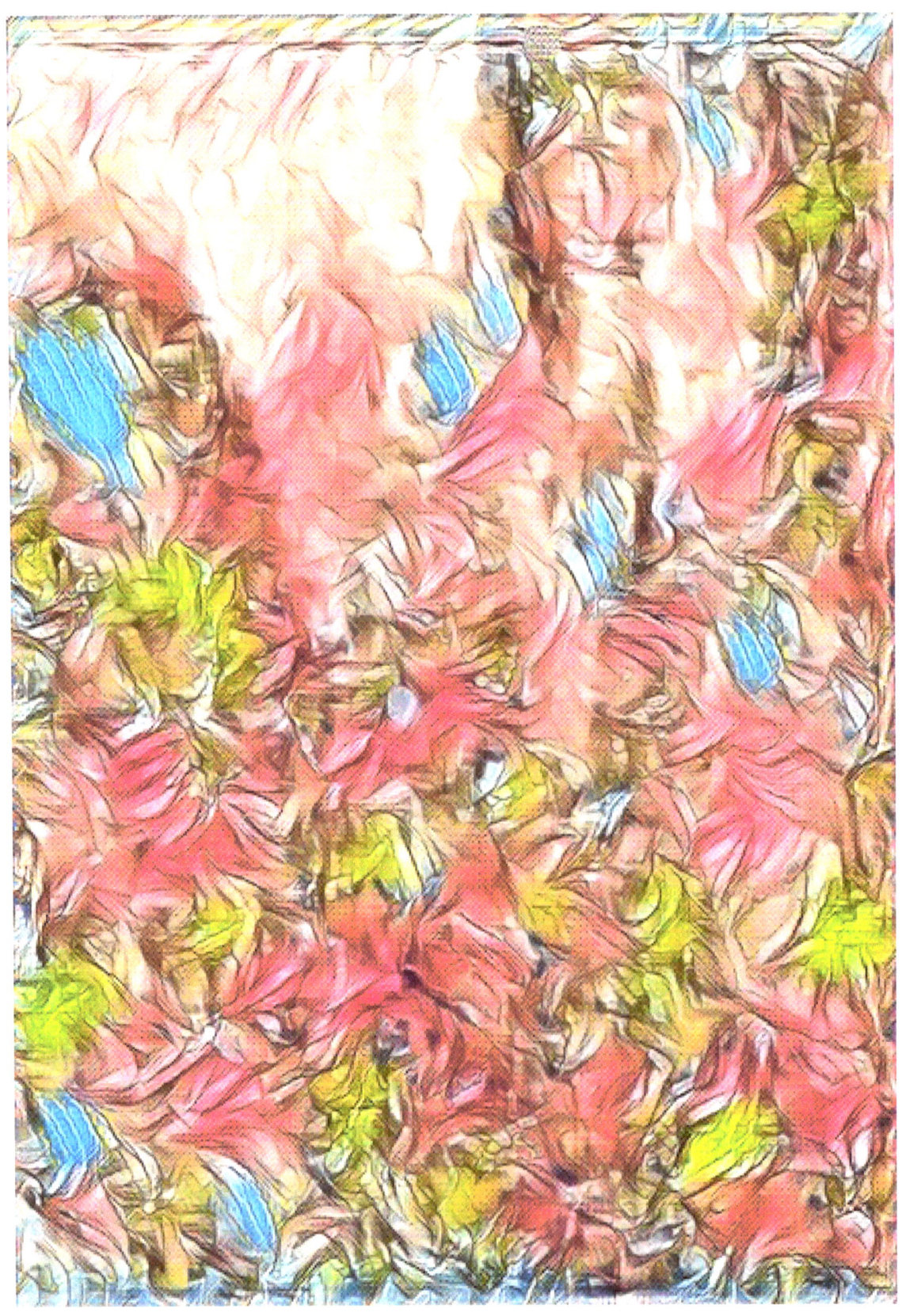

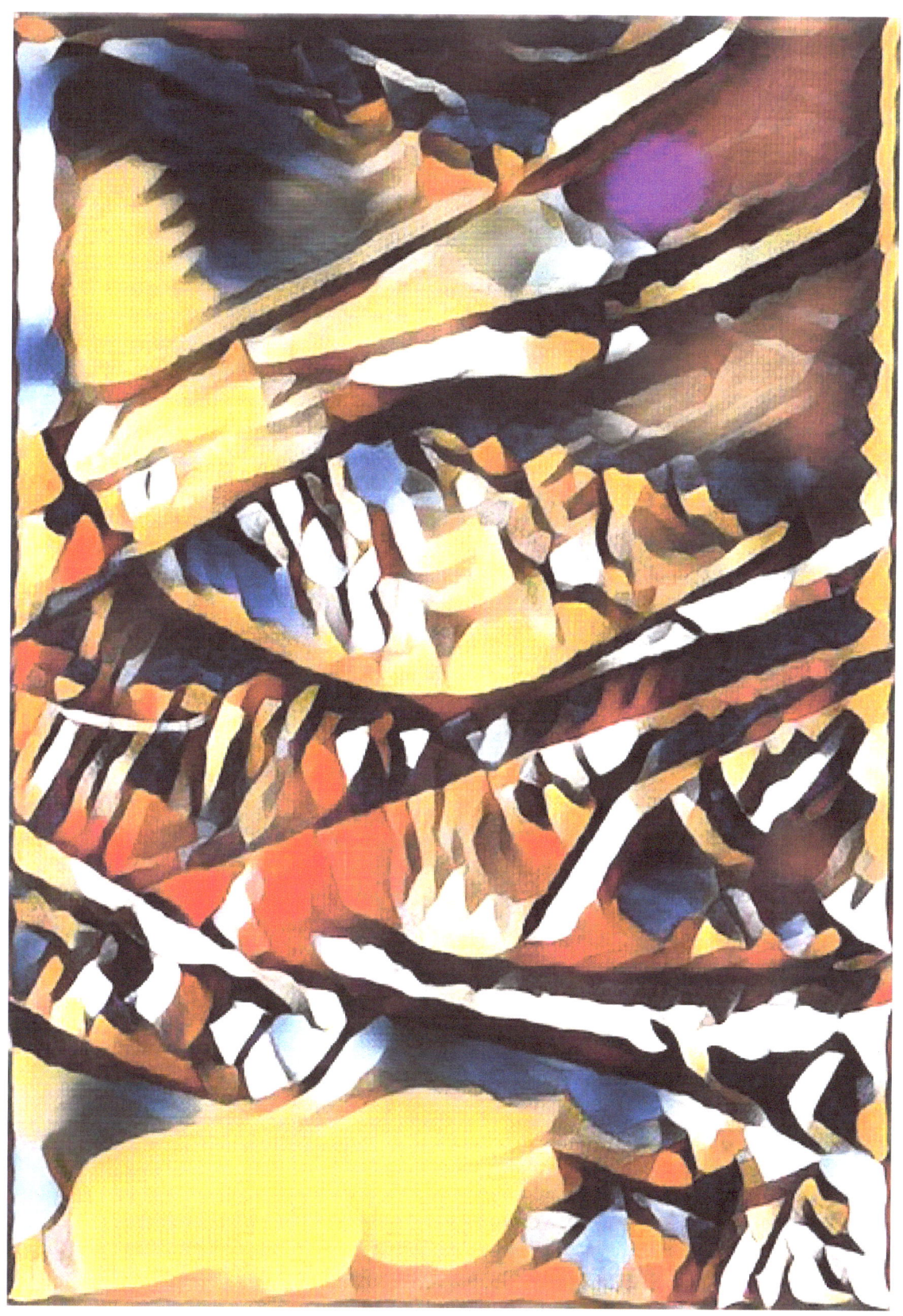

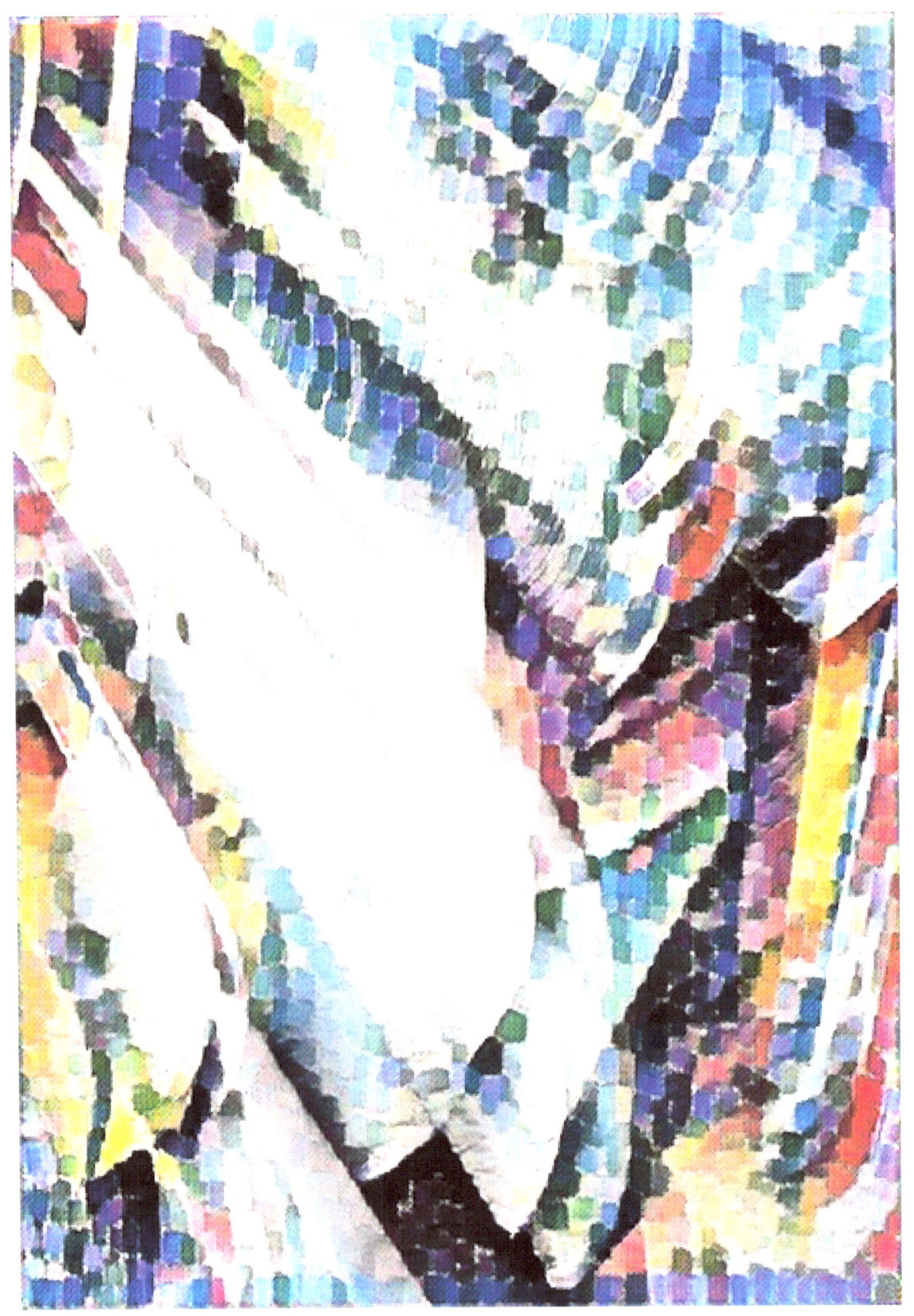

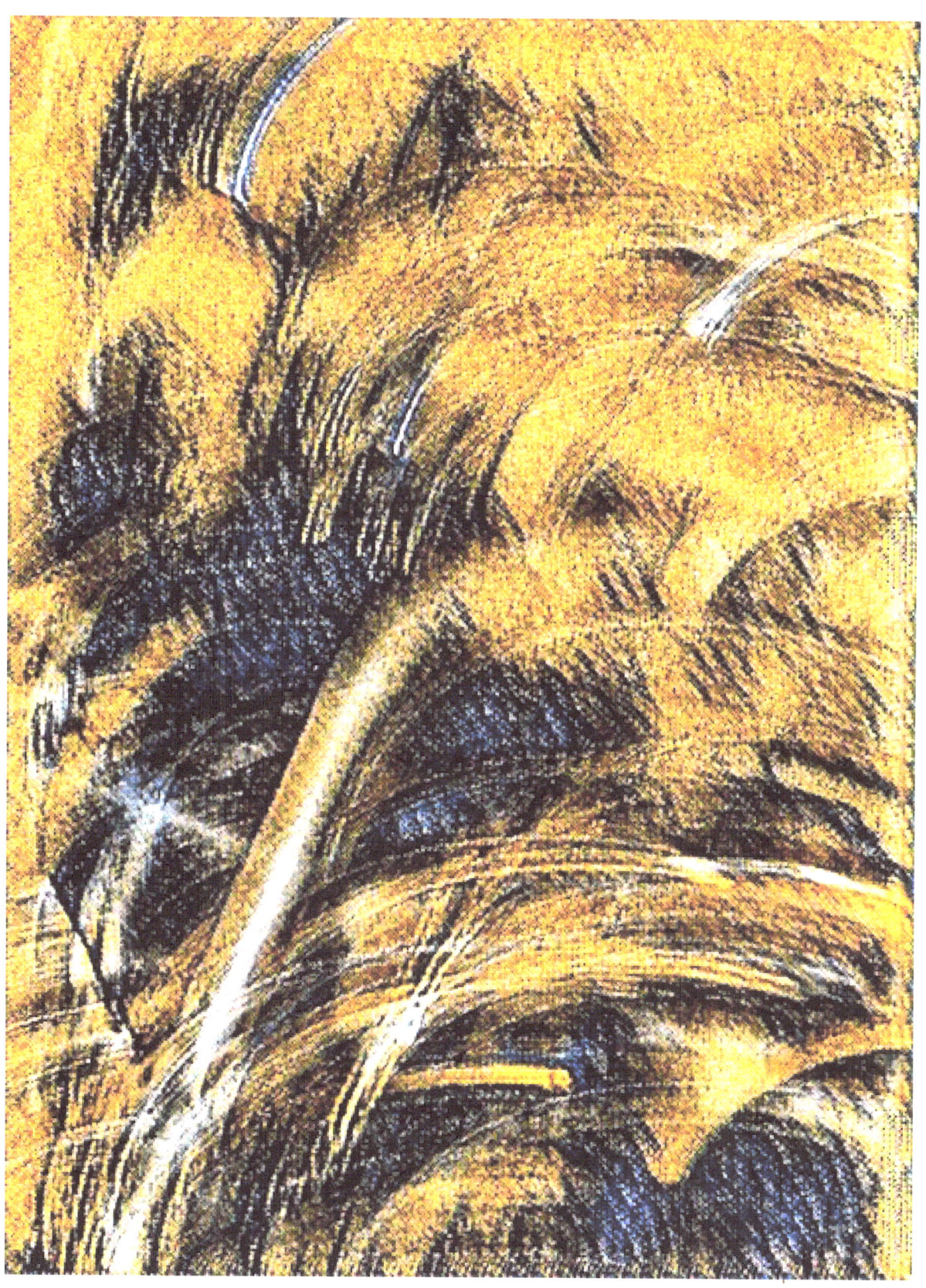